A STUDY IN GENIUS

Master Drawings and Watercolours from the Collection of Her Majesty the Queen in the Royal Library, Windsor Castle

Jane Roberts

Art Gallery of New South Wales, Sydney
1 June–17 July 1988

National Gallery of Victoria, Melbourne
29 July–11 September 1988

Queensland Art Gallery, Brisbane
23 September–6 November 1988

The Art Gallery of New South Wales Trust wishes
to acknowledge the most generous support of

Her Majesty the Queen
The Royal Library, Windsor Castle
Department of the Arts, Sport, the Environment,
Tourism and Territories
British Airways

© Her Majesty the Queen
Copyright reserved
The drawings are reproduced
by gracious permission of
Her Majesty Queen Elizabeth II.

Published by the Art Gallery of New South Wales, Sydney
ISBN-0-7305-5517-8
Second Edition

CATALOGUE DESIGN
Spatchurst Design Associates

PRINTING
Beaver Press

TYPESETTING
InterType Pty Ltd

INDEMNIFIED BY THE AUSTRALIAN GOVERNMENT
THROUGH THE DEPARTMENT OF THE ARTS, SPORT, THE ENVIRONMENT,
TOURISM AND TERRITORIES

SPONSORED BY

BRITISH AIRWAYS
The world's favourite airline.

Contents

Foreword	4
Preface	5
Introduction	7
List of Works referred to in abbreviated form	12
Catalogue	
Italian Renaissance (nos. 1-21)	14
Northern Renaissance (nos. 22-27)	56
Seventeenth Century (nos. 28-40)	68
Eighteenth and Nineteenth Centuries (nos. 41-50)	94
Artists' Biographies	114
Index of Artists	120

Foreword

Through the generosity of Her Majesty The Queen, Australia has been privileged to see in recent years three exhibitions from the Royal Library, all of which were devoted to the drawings of Leonardo da Vinci. The present exhibition is a rather more ambitious project in that it is the first to be held in Australia that includes examples of virtually the full chronological range of drawings and watercolours in the Royal Collection: from the Italian Renaissance to the 19th Century. The fifty works selected are rich in individual quality but, furthermore, they illustrate the sustained excellence of the Royal Collections.

The magnificence of the Renaissance is shown in the ten drawings of Leonardo, which illustrate his extraordinary range of interests, his vision and the exquisiteness of his drawing; in Raphael there is a sense of completeness as though even the sketch is a final consummate statement; and in Michelangelo there is indelible power and strength, whilst works by Perugino, Sebastiano and Salviati illustrate further the Renaissance achievement. Holbein's majestic and unerring portraits are very different; here there is that sense of definition and commitment of the Northern Renaissance. It is a quality to be seen also in the clarity of the drawing of Durer and the fantastic imagery of Hirschvogel, which is in some contrast to the sheer emotive vigour of the 17th century drawings of Annibale Carracci, Guido Reni and Guercino. The sense of classicism is then restored in the works of Claude Lorrain, Nicolas Poussin and Canaletto. The final group in the selection is of English artists, Sanby, Harding, Nash and Simpson, all of which concentrate with characteristic quiet persuasion, on architectural themes.

For this exhibition of such undoubted quality we are indebted to Her Majesty The Queen for permitting these works to travel to Australia in the Bicentennial Year.

We express our thanks to the Librarian, Oliver Everett, to the Curator of the Print Room, the Honourable Mrs. Jane Roberts, who wrote the catalogue, to the Assistant Curator–Exhibitions, Miss Theresa-Mary Morton and to all at the Royal Library who have been associated with the planning and preparation of this exhibition. We must also acknowledge the generous support of our sponsor, British Airways, for without them we simply could not afford to present such a marvellous exhibition.

We acknowledge too with gratitude the indemnity provision offered by the Australian Government through the Department of Arts, Sport, the Environment, Tourism and Territories.

Finally my thanks to my colleagues at the National Gallery of Victoria and the Queensland Art Gallery for their co-operation in participating in the tour of 'A Study in Genius: Master Drawings and Watercolours from the Collection of Her Majesty The Queen'.

Edmund Capon
Director,
Art Gallery of New South Wales

PREFACE

From early 1985, discussions took place between representatives of the British Royal Collection and the Australian Bicentennial Authority. The hope was that one way in which the Bicentenary in 1988 might be very well marked and celebrated would be with an exhibition in Australia of items from Her Majesty The Queen's Collection of art treasures. The current exhibition of Master Drawings and Watercolours from the Royal Collection is the result of that original idea. The project has had the warm approval of Her Majesty The Queen from its inception.

The Royal Collection of Drawings and Watercolours is housed in the Royal Library at Windsor Castle. It is one of the most distinguished and important such collections in the world. Items from it have been seen in Australia before but never has there been an exhibition there which seeks to represent the very wide range of the Collection. Previous exhibitions have concentrated on the works of a single artist, notably Leonardo da Vinci. By contrast, the current exhibition covers the range from the Italian Renaissance, the Northern Renaissance, Seventeenth-century master draughtsmen through to the Eighteenth and Nineteenth centuries finishing with some striking watercolours of Royal Residences in Britain.

It is very difficult in a selection of 50 drawings and watercolours to represent fully or fairly a collection comprising over thirty thousand items. Nevertheless, the 27 artists whose works are shown include a remarkable number of famous names and give an excellent idea of the extent of the collection.

Prime credit for the selection and for the writing of this catalogue goes to Jane Roberts, Curator of the Print Room in the Royal Library. Her first exhibition representing the full range of the collection was shown in The Queen's Gallery, Buckingham Palace, from February 1986 to April 1987. It consisted of 149 drawings and watercolours. The current exhibition for the Australian Bicentenary does not include any of those shown in The Queen's Gallery but has a similar objective.

Patrick McCaughey, former Director of the National Gallery of Victoria, who was very much involved in the evolution of the current exhibition, saw that original Queen's Gallery exhibition and considered with our full agreement that a similar concept should be the basis of this display.

The Royal Library on behalf of the Royal Collection has much appreciated and enjoyed the help and cooperation concerning this exhibition that it has received from Edmund Capon, Director of the Art Gallery of New South Wales, Sydney; Nancy Staub, Deputy Director (Public Programs) at the National Gallery of Victoria; and Dr. Caroline Turner, Deputy Director, Manager International Programs, of the Queensland Art Gallery, Brisbane. Thanks are also due to particular members of the Royal Library staff in addition to Jane Roberts: Julia Baxter, Theresa-Mary Morton, Michael Warnes, Julian Clare, Eva Zielinska-Millar and Olive Fortey.

OLIVER EVERETT
Librarian, Windsor Castle
November 1987

Introduction

The fifty drawings and watercolours in this exhibition have been selected to represent the extent and the main strengths of the Royal Collection, which include a total of around thirty thousand drawings and watercolours. The Collection has grown and developed steadily over many hundreds of years. Although records are incomplete for the sixteenth and seventeenth centuries, we know that already by 1690 the eighty or so drawings by Holbein (including Nos. 24–26), and the unsurpassed group of studies by Leonardo da Vinci (including Nos. 4–13) had entered the Collection. In both cases the drawings were housed in large albums until some time in the last century. It was only natural therefore that they should be kept in the Royal Library alongside other manuscript and printed material. The Royal Collection of drawings and watercolours has been relocated (with the Library) on a number of occasions, from Whitehall to St James's, Kensington, Buckingham House (then Palace), and finally Windsor, where the Royal Library has been established for the last 150 years. The Print Room in Windsor Castle, where all the items in this exhibition are normally to be found, was arranged and decorated according to the orders of the Prince Consort, within the last two years of his life (1860-61), and has remained unchanged (externally at any rate) since that time.

Drawings and watercolours have been collected and treasured for many centuries. The first so-called 'collections' were made by the artists themselves. Particularly before the invention of photography and high quality printing methods, the only way of recording the appearance of things (whether the outer features or inner structure of the human body, an elaborate hairstyle, a plant, or an animal) was to make (or to acquire) a sketch of it. The normal stock-in-trade of an artist's workshop would have included countless drawings of the same type as No. 2. The use to which they were put makes it truly remarkable that they have survived to our own day, around five hundred years later.

On his death in 1519 Leonardo's drawings were bequeathed to his favourite pupil, Francesco Melzi. The path by which the Leonardo drawings now at Windsor entered the Royal Collection is a long and complicated one (see summarised provenance in the entry for No. 4). For our present purposes, it is sufficient to mention that among those through whose hands they passed was the sculptor, Pompeo Leoni. The numerous drawings of Parmigianino were also often acquired by fellow-artists. One of them was mounted into a drawing by Ludovico Carracci (No. 28) at an early stage. A number of notable British artists, from Lely to Paul Sandby and Thomas Lawrence, formed important collections of Old Master Drawings, which are now scattered through the great museums and art galleries of the world.

The British monarchs have collected drawings from the seventeenth century at least, but although contemporary inventories mention drawings, none can be positively identified today. Nicholas Lanier is said to have applied a large star mark to those

LEFT: DETAIL CAT NO. 48

INTRODUCTION

items that he acquired for Charles I (d. 1649) and a smaller mark (see No. 19) to those he acquired for Thomas Howard, Earl of Arundel (d. 1646). Drawings bearing both marks are to be found in most great collections. However, those drawings in the Royal Collection which can be traced back with some certainty to the seventeenth century are invariably unmarked. These include works by Raphael and Michelangelo in addition to the Leonardos and Holbeins.

Following the Hanoverian succession in 1714 the purchasing of works of art was temporarily at a standstill. However, George II's eldest son, Frederick, Prince of Wales (d. 1751), was an enlightened patron and collector and acquired items such as the Massimi Poussin drawings (including No. 35 and part of No. 37) from the great connoisseur Dr Richard Mead. It remained to Prince Frederick's eldest son, who succeeded to the throne as George III in 1760, to prompt the massive purchases of drawings which have made the Royal Collection one of the major repositories of graphic art in the world.

Through his agents in Italy, the King was able to acquire two vast collections. The first (which cost £20,000) consisted of the paintings, drawings, prints, books, coins and gems belonging to Joseph Smith, one-time British Consul in Venice. The second (which cost a mere £3,500) comprised the drawing and print collection of Cardinal Allessandro Albani. The first consignment included the 143 drawings by Canaletto (eg. Nos. 41–43), the 209 studies by Sebastiano Ricci, and the 36 framed heads by Piazzetta (eg. No. 44). In addition there were several volumes of drawings and prints by Castiglione (including No. 34) from the collection of Zaccaria Sagredo (d. 1729), and a number of other sixteenth and seventeenth century drawings (eg. Nos. 28 and 30) which can be traced in the Bonfiglioli inventory c.1700 and which later passed to Smith via Sagredo. The second (Albani) collection was also composed of a number of different sections: the *museo cartaceo* (paper museum) of the early seventeenth-century scholar Cassiano dal Pozzo; the Albani 'drawings archive', consisting of drawings (particularly architectural drawings, by Carlo Fontana, etc.) by artists patronised by the family; and lastly the great body of material purchased from the artist Carlo Maratta in 1703, which included that artist's 200 drawings now at Windsor (eg. No. 33) as well as those by his master Andrea Sacchi, and the vast groups of studies by Domenichino and members of the Carracci family. In addition to these purchases from the Smith and Albani collections the King continued to buy in Italy throughout the first two decades of his reign. However by the time the great inventory of drawings was made c.1800 ('Inventory A') all specific evidence of provenance had been lost. Although it has been possible to find a reference in Inventory A for almost every one of the old master drawings (both northern and southern) here discussed, it is often difficult to go any further back into their history. For instance, Perugino's *Head of the Virgin* (No. 3) was said to have been acquired in Rome. Where and when we are not told. The bringing together of drawings by the

INTRODUCTION

same artist which had formerly been divided between different collections had a number of beneficial side-effects. For instance, Poussin's drawing of 'the Agony in the Garden' (No. 37) was divided across the middle during the seventeenth century, for some unknown reason. The lower half had passed through the collections of Cardinal Massimi, Richard Mead and Frederick Prince of Wales before reaching George III's collection. With that monarch's purchase of the Albani drawings in 1762 it could be (and now has been) united with the upper half once more.

Paul Sandby was an almost exact contemporary of George III and was employed as drawing master to some of his children, but the King appears to have owned very few works by the master. One of the most notable early collectors of Sandby's work was the scientist Sir Joseph Banks, well-known for his activities in sponsoring agricultural and natural historical projects and for his voyages of discovery, but less so for his art collecting. The wonderful view of the Lower Ward of Windsor Castle (No. 45) was only acquired for the Royal Collection in 1876, at the sale of Banks' collection by one of his descendants.

During the last decades of the nineteenth century small numbers of old master drawings were purchased for the Collection largely through London auctioneers and dealers. But throughout Queen Victoria's reign the main emphasis was on the commissioning of accurate views of houses, events, or portraits of members of the family or friends (eg. Nos. 47-50). In the present century the Collection has continued to grow, but the main activity has been the cataloguing and conserving of this great body of drawings. In recent years a number of exhibitions consisting entirely of material from the Print Room have been staged around the world, thus allowing a total of well over three million people to be granted access (however temporarily) to the Royal Collection.

Because of its great age and importance it would be interesting to know how much access was granted to the drawings during the last two hundred or so years, but such information is not readily available. The appearance of certain old master drawings was, however, disseminated from the seventeenth century via printed copies. Wenceslaus Hollar's series of etchings of items in Lord Arundel's collection included one of Leonardo's drawing of a child (No. 7). A hundred years later, Francesco Bartolozzi was granted permission to make engraved copies of some of George III's drawings, such as Maratta's design in honour of Pietro da Cortona (No. 33). John Chamberlaine's *Original Designs . . . in His Majesty's Collection* (London, 1812) contains high quality actual size reproductions engraved by F. C. and G. Lewis, and by P. W. Tomkins, of drawings by Leonardo, Raphael, and Claude among those selected here (see Nos. 4, 5, 17 and 38-40). In the same year the Holbein drawings (including Nos. 24-26) were published in a popular quarto edition, also by

INTRODUCTION

Chamberlaine, following the success of his larger folio edition of *Imitations of Original Drawings by Hans Holbein,* issued 1792-1800. Joseph Nash's fine colour plates after his own watercolours (eg. No. 48) were made for a rather different purpose, and well demonstrate the skill and ingenuity of the nineteenth-century printmakers.

Meanwhile with Thurston Thompson's series of photographs of the Raphael drawings at Windsor, published with the Prince Consort's active encouragement in 1857, the study of connoisseurship and art history entered a new epoch, in which an accurate knowledge of the appearance of an object could be obtained with comparative ease. For many years it has been the case that the Windsor Print Room (and other similar establishments) receives considerably more requests for photographs than for appointments to study the drawings at first hand. Photography, and printed illustrations based on this photography, has provided the foundation for work on the series of published catalogues covering the Windsor drawings, as summarised on page 12. All but the last five items in this exhibition have thus been made known to scholars. The nineteenth century catalogue is in an active state of preparation, and I have been fortunate to be able to discuss the entries for Nos. 47-50 with the author of that catalogue, Delia Millar. I have discussed other catalogue entries with Diane de Grazia, Michael Hirst and A.V.B. Norman, all of whom have provided helpful suggestions.

One of the aspects of interest to drawings scholars that is virtually impossible without access to the originals is the study of techniques. All the main traditional drawing techniques were used by the artists of the Italian Renaissance, developing the methods of the scribes and illuminators in their use of metalpoint (Nos. 3, 4, 6 and 14), white heightening (Nos. 1, 14, etc.) and of course pen and ink (Nos. 2, 5, 10, 11, etc.). By the end of the fifteenth century black and red chalk was also being used to give a greater feeling of volume, movement and structure than had been possible with the much less versatile metalpoint (Nos. 7, 8, 9, 12, 13, 15, 16, 18, etc.). The addition of wash to a pen and ink drawing was also used to provide increasingly dramatic effects of light and shade (Nos. 2, 20 and 21), which were later fully exploited by the artists of the Baroque era (Nos. 28, 30, 31). Such drawings act as a fitting preparation for Canaletto's use of monochrome wash (eg. Nos. 41-3), and thus for the work of the English watercolourists, such as Paul Sandby (Nos. 45 and 46). By the middle of the nineteenth century watercolour (with additions of bodycolour) was being used in a very different way in a method partly derived from oil painting practice. The present selection also includes one of the strange 'painted drawings' of Castiglione (No. 34).

All the drawings and watercolours in this exhibition are on paper, which is almost invariably cream coloured. However, the anonymous study with which it opens is an early example of a work on blue paper (No. 1), while Piazzetta's drawings

INTRODUCTION

(eg. No. 44) were also once on blue-grey paper, now faded to a dull buff. The early metalpoint drawings are executed on paper coated with a coloured preparation.

These different techniques are only partly explained by the variety of purposes for which the drawings were intended. These could be divided into three broad categories: life studies, drawings for specific projects, and finished works of art. However, few drawings can be so easily typecast. Leonardo's plant studies (eg. No. 12) are both more and less than life drawings. On the one hand they are the earliest scientifically observed botanical diagrams, and on the other they were probably partly carried out in order to provide the artist with a vocabulary of plant types for inclusion in the foreground of his paintings. Raphael's drawing of Leda (No. 17) is confusingly not an original design, but a copy of one by Leonardo (with which his No. 11 is also closely related). Holbein's portrait drawings (Nos. 24–6) must, from their brief colour annotations, have been made from the life in preparation for larger scale works in oil, but no autograph paintings relating to any of the three exhibited drawings are known. And so on.

Within the second category (drawings for specific projects), Perugino's study of a female head (No. 3) is directly preparatory for the figure of the Virgin in an altarpiece by the master. Leonardo's Neptune (No. 8) is related to a documented finished drawing, while the extraordinary rearing horse in red chalk (No. 9) must be connected to his mural painting of the *Battle of Anghiari*. The drawings of Filippino and Sebastiano (Nos. 14 and 19) are more distantly related to known works, while Raphael's warrior shielding his eyes (No. 18) was for an unexecuted altarpiece commission. The studies by both Lelio Orsi and Annibale Carracci were made in preparation for fresco projects, the former (No. 21) exterior, the latter (No. 29) interior. At least one of the exhibited drawings appears to have been made as a preparatory study for an engraving rather than a painting (No. 22).

Within the area of finished drawings we should include Salviati's altarpiece design (No. 20), which was presumably made for the approval of the prospective patron prior to the commencement of more detailed work on the project. The Dürer *Virgin and Child* and Hirschvogel *Crucifixion* (Nos. 23 and 27) share a degree of finish which makes it hard to accept that they were not considered adequate as works of art in their own right. The same was certainly the case for each of the last ten items in the exhibition.

Leonardo wrote that more can be conveyed in a drawing than in a thousand words. It is to be hoped that the visitors to this exhibition will agree.

JANE ROBERTS
Windsor
November 1987

List of Works Referred to in Abbreviated Form

Bartsch A. Bartsch, *Le Peintre Graveur,* Vienna, 1803-21

BC A. Blunt, *The Drawings of G. B. Castiglione and Stefano della Bella in the Collection of Her Majesty The Queen at Windsor Castle,* London, 1954

BF A. Blunt, *The French Drawings in the Collection of His Majesty The King at Windsor Castle,* London, 1945

BM A. Blunt, *Supplements to the Catalogues of Italian and French Drawings in the Collection of Her Majesty The Queen at Windsor Castle,* London, 1971

BR A. Blunt and H. L. Cooke, *The Roman Drawings of the XVII and XVIII Centuries in the Collection of Her Majesty The Queen at Windsor Castle,* London, 1960

Briquet C. M. Briquet, *Les Filigranes,* Paris, 1907

BV A. Blunt and E. Croft-Murray, *Venetian Drawings of the XVII and XVIII Centuries in the Collection of Her Majesty The Queen at Windsor Castle,* London, 1957

C&P K. Clark and C. Pedretti, *The Drawings of Leonardo da Vinci at Windsor Castle,* London, 1968-9

C/L W. G. Constable, *Canaletto* (2nd edn., revised by J. G. Links) London, 1976

Heawood E. Heawood, *Watermarks...of the Seventeenth and Eighteenth Centuries,* Hilversum, 1950

Inv. A The larger of the two inventories listing the drawings in the Royal Collection during the latter part of the reign of George III (Windsor Castle, Print Room)

K/P K. Keele and C. Pedretti, *Leonardo da Vinci: Corpus of the Anatomical Studies...at Windsor Castle,* London and New York, 1979-80

Lugt F. Lugt, *Les marques de collections de dessins et d'estampes,* Amsterdam, 1921; *Supplément,* The Hague, 1956

M&T D. Mahon and N. Turner, *The Drawings by Guercino in the Collection of Her Majesty The Queen at Windsor Castle,* Cambridge, 1988 (forthcoming)

Oppé A. P. Oppé, *English Drawings...in the Collection of His Majesty The King at Windsor Castle,* London, 1950

P&W A. E. Popham and J. Wilde, *The Italian Drawings of the XV and XVI Centuries in the Collection of His Majesty The King at Windsor Castle,* London 1949; reprinted, with an Appendix by R. Wood, New York, 1985

PC K. T. Parker, *The Drawings of Antonio Canaletto in the Collection of His Majesty The King at Windsor Castle,* London, 1948

Pedretti *The Drawings and Miscellaneous Papers of Leonardo da Vinci...at Windsor Castle* ed. C. Pedretti, New York and London, 1981-

PH K. T. Parker, *The Drawings of Hans Holbein in the Collection of His Majesty The King at Windsor Castle,* London, 1945; reprinted, with an Appendix by S. Foister, New York, 1983

RL Inventory of the drawings in the Royal Library, Windsor Castle

W R. Wittkower, *The Drawings of the Carracci in the Collection of Her Majesty The Queen at Windsor Castle,* London, 1952

Note

The following entries are divided into the broad categories of the Italian Renaissance (Nos. 1-21), the Northern Renaissance (Nos. 22-27), the Seventeenth century (Nos. 28-40) and the Eighteenth and Nineteenth centuries (Nos. 41-50). Within those categories the work of each artist is ordered chronologically within the artist's *oeuvre,* and the various artists are discussed chronologically according to their dates of birth. Measurements are given height before width.

Catalogue

Attributed to BENOZZO GOZZOLI (c.1421-1497)

1 *Seated youth drawing, and sleeping dog,*
c.1480/90

237 x 179 mm.
Drawn and modelled with the
brush in black wash, heightened with white,
on blue paper.

Verso. Study of an ox (inverted).
Black chalk heightened with white.

Unlike the other early drawings in this exhibition, the present sheet appears to be unrelated to a finished composition, and to have been drawn purely to record an everyday scene: a young scribe (or draughtsman?) at work, and a dog curled up asleep. The animal study on the *verso* is likewise merely a hasty record, drawn from the life.

A number of different attributions have been proposed, ranging from Masaccio to Davide Ghirlandaio (Berenson). Popham described it as 'Anonymous Florentine', while Degenhart & Schmitt attribute it to an artist influenced by the late style of Benozzo Gozzoli.

The use of blue paper (*carta azzurra*) by Renaissance artists was more prevalent in Venice and the Veneto than in Florence. If the attribution is correct, this must represent one of the first Tuscan uses of the material. The sheet has been repaired along both the left and the right sides.

Provenance: George III (Inv. A, p.14. 'Albert Dürer e Maestri Antrichi Div:si. 12: Man writing with a Dog')

Literature: P&W 33; B. Degenhart Degenhart and A. Schmitt, *Corpus der Italienischen Zeichnungen 1300-1450, I: Süd und Mittelitalien,* Berlin, 1968, I, ii, 474; RL 12796

School of MANTEGNA (late fifteenth century)

2   *Sheet of studies with a seated soldier,* 1479

247 x 189 mm.
Pen and brown ink, and brown, grey and white wash applied with brush, over rubbed (? or offset) black and red chalk.

Verso. Architectural and drapery studies. Pen and ink, black chalk and grey wash, heightened with white.

The drawings on both *recto* and *verso* of this sheet are typical products of a north Italian painter's workshop of the second half of the fifteenth century. An interest in classical antiquity is evident in the seated soldier (in Roman dress) on the *recto* and also in the architectural detail on the *verso*.

It is likely that the main study on the *recto*, and the shadowy standing figure behind him, were copied from a painting by Mantegna of a subject from Christ's Passion (for instance, Christ rising from the tomb), although the prototype has yet to be found. Compare, however, the pose of the main figure with that of the soldier seated (in reverse) in the foreground of the *Resurrection* from Mantegna's San Zeno altarpiece (Musée des Beaux-Arts, Tours). The ink sketches top left may also relate to a Passion series.

Popham identified the work of at least two, and possibly three, hands among the studies on this sheet. A closely related page, possibly from the same sketchbook, is in the Boymans Museum, Rotterdam. It contains similarly abbreviated pen and ink figure sketches, the legs terminating in points rather than feet. The Rotterdam sheet bears a fragmentary inscription and the date 1479. A third related study was in the Wauters Collection (see *Le Dessin Italien dans les Collections Hollandaises*, exh. cat., Paris etc., 1962, No. 24).

Provenance: George III (Inv. A, p.14: 'Albert Dürer e Maestri Antichi Div:si, p. 17: a very stiff figure in Armour')

Literature: P&W 16; RL 12795

PIETRO PERUGINO (c.1445-1523)

3 *Head of the Virgin,* 1493

233 x 224 mm.
Metalpoint heightened with white on paper coated with a pale salmon pink preparation.
Watermark: rearing horse or stag (fragmentary).

This drawing has long been recognised as a preparatory study for the head of the Virgin in Perugino's altarpiece from San Domenico, Fiesole, now in the Uffizi, Florence (No. 1435). The painting dates from 1493 and shows the Virgin and Child seated under a loggia between Saints John the Baptist and Sebastian.

Although badly rubbed, the firm outlines of the face, neck and shoulders have remained clearly legible. The shape of the veiled head is less easily visible, as all but the shading lines above the ear have disappeared. Perugino has subtly altered the hairstyle in the painting, so that falling ringlets break up the neckline and match the falling hair already shown to the right of the Virgin's neck in the drawing. Otherwise this study has been followed in all essentials in the finished picture.

Provenance: George III (Inv. A, p.50: 'Raffaello d'Urbino e Scuola, p.12: A Head. Great Expression, but much damaged; in the same Collection as No.17. The latter, P&W 803, is described as having been 'bought at Rome')

Literature: P&W 22; F. Ames Lewis and J. Wright, *Drawing in the Italian Renaissance Workshop*, exh. cat., Nottingham and London, 1983, No.73, RL 12744

LEONARDO DA VINCI (1452-1519)

4 *Female portrait in profile,* c.1480/90

318 x 199 mm (irregular).
Metalpoint on buff prepared paper.

This study was drawn in the tradition of earlier Renaissance portraits, with a pure profile akin to the likenesses found on antique coins and thence introduced to portrait medals. However Leonardo has imbued his sitter with a degree of solemnity and particularly a three-dimensionality which is seldom found in Italian profile portraits. The drawing was presumably intended to be worked up into a painting (or possibly a sculptural relief), but no directly related work is known. The identity of the sitter is likewise unknown. Her modest head-dress appears more Florentine than Milanese, which would suggest a date before c.1483 when Leonardo moved to Milan. There are few points of reference to assist us in precisely locating his metalpoint drawings between the mid-1470s and 1495 when he ceased to use this medium. This drawing, for instance, has similarities in the handling of the metalpoint with the horse studies (such as No.6) carried out in Milan c.1490, but it could well have been drawn around a decade earlier.

Provenance: Francesco Melzi; Pompeo Leoni; Thomas Howard, Earl of Arundel; (?) King Charles I; Royal Collection since 1690 at least.

Literature: C&P: Pedretti III, 163; RL 12505

LEONARDO DA VINCI (1452-1519)

5   *An artillery park*, c.1487

250 x 183 mm.
Pen and ink

This incident-filled drawing appears to show a courtyard with a cannon store. In the centre a vast cannon is lifted into place on a gun carriage by a crane. To right and left teams of naked men strain at levers which turn the axles to which the crane cables are attached. Another team manoeuvres the front of the carriage into place under the barrel. In the foreground is the bed in which the cannon had formerly been housed. It is still resting on its rollers. Behind the main scene, which occupies everyone present, a number of other cannon on similar beds are shown in a lean-to store abutting the castellated outer wall of a fortress. Cannon balls, also of various sizes, poles and ladders, complete the scene.

Stylistically the drawing must be dated to Leonardo's first Milanese visit, c.1483-99, during which time he was employed in various capacities by the Sforza rulers of Milan. When he first offered his services to Ludovico Sforza he wrote in the following words: 'Most illustrious Lord, having now fully studied the work of all those who claim to be masters and artificers of instruments of war . . . I will lay before your Lordship my secret inventions and then offer to carry them into execution 'at your pleasure'. He was evidently no stranger to scenes such as that depicted on this drawing.

Provenance: see No.4 (George III, Inv. A, p.27: Leonardo, vol.3, p.18, 'A great number of Men raising with a Quadrangular Machine & placing it on its Carriage. A very large & one of the first invented pieces of Ordnance exactly similar to those on the Europe side of the Dardanelles with a view of many pieces of various proportions, in the same style, with Mortars, Bomb Shells, Carriages &c . . . With a Pen')

Literature: C&P; Pedretti IV, RL 12647

Leonardo da Vinci (1452-1519)

6   *Right profile of a horse, c.1490*

212 x 159 mm.
Metalpoint on blue prepared paper.
Inscribed (in reverse) on horse's chest
to right: *a b*, and along lower edge:
a b quáto el pie (a b is as much as the foot).

The horse played a central part in a number of Leonardo's commissions from the early *Adoration* to the late Trivulzio monument. It is not surprising therefore that a large number of studies by Leonardo of horses have survived. This drawing was evidently made from the life, but the inscriptions and the vertical and horizontal lines added to the main figure indicate that it was then used for the application of Leonardo's ideas concerning the unified system of proportions which he believed could be found in the bodies of animals, as in humans.

The technique of this drawing suggests a dating before c.1495, when Leonardo abandoned the use of metalpoint. Kenneth Clark considered it 'one of the most exquisite, and perhaps one of the last', of Leonardo's drawings in this medium. It belongs to his intensive study of horses in Milan (1482-9 in connection with the commission for an equestrian monument to commemorate Francesco Sforza. The pose finally selected for the horse in this monument was not dissimilar from that shown here.

Provenance: see under No.4 (possibly identifiable in George III, Inv. A, p.36: Leonardo, vol.3, p.166, among 2 Horses – blue paper – neat)

Literature: C&P: Pedretti II, 92; RL 12321

Leonardo da Vinci (1452-1519)

7 *Head and shoulders of a child, in profile,* late 1490s

100 x 100 mm.
Red chalk.

At first glance, this drawing appears to be a closely observed life study of a child, showing the loose folds of skin in the neck and under the armpits characteristic of young childhood. Another drawing at Windsor (RL 12567) appears to show the same child, equally closely observed, but now from the front and back and omitting the head.

Parallels have been pointed out between the appearance and position of this child and the infant Christ in the London version of the *Virgin of the Rocks*. However, the complex relationship between that picture and the earlier version (in the Louvre) has otherwise suggested that Leonardo did not carry out detailed studies for the later picture. In the Louvre version the head of the infant Christ is slightly tilted towards the spectator.

The way in which the child's figure is cut off, in horizontal section, below the shoulder is so unlike Leonardo's other figure drawings (such as Nos.4 and 11) that a possible connection with a piece of sculpture has been suggested. In the late sixteenth century Lomazzo mentioned a small head and the Christ Child in terra cotta by Leonardo (*Trattato della Pittura*, Milan, 1584, II, viii, p.127). In spite of Leonardo's early training in the workshop of Verrocchio, and a number of known commissions for sculptural projects (see, for instance, No.6), no piece of sculpture definitely from his hand appears to have survived. The red chalk technique of this drawing would seem to date it to the late 1490s. The reason for the fading of the chalk at the back of the child's head is not known.

Provenance: see under No.4.

Literature: C&P: Pedretti III, 189; RL 12519

Leonardo da Vinci (1452-1519)

8   *Neptune with four sea horses*, c.1503/04

251 x 391 mm.
Black chalk. Inscribed along upper edge:
abassi i chavalli (lower the horses).

Neptune, the god of the sea, rides in an almost invisible shell chariot, holding the reins of his sea-horses (with heads and forelegs of horses, and tails of fish) as they rear up and lash out to either side. His trident (three-pronged fork) is raised up. In the foreground two dolphins are lightly sketched in.

This study is self-evidently related to a (lost) drawing of the same subject, well-known in the early sources and described by the sixteenth-century biographer Vasari as having been presented by Leonardo to his good friend Antonio Segni. As such it may have been the first instance of a new type of artefact, the highly finished 'presentation drawing', as well-represented in Michelangelo's *oeuvre* of the 1520s and 1530s. The subject-matter for these drawings was often taken from classical mythology. Appropriately the stance of the main figures in this study was derived from a sarcophagus now in the Vatican. Segni's drawing was frequently copied in the sixteenth century.

The appearance of this preparatory study is quite unlike the highly finished form of Segni's gift. The impression of pent-up energy, and of fear and tension in the horse's heads, conveyed with an extraordinary fluidity, closely resembles Leonardo's drawings for the wall-painting of the *Battle of Anghiari* for the Palazzo Vecchio, Florence, on which he was working between 1503 and 1505. The Neptune drawing was presumably worked on at the same time, and would have been presented prior to Segni's departure for Rome in 1504. The inscription presumably indicates that Leonardo intended that Neptune should stand proud of his sea-horses.

Provenance: see under No.4 (George III, Inv. A, p.36: Leonardo, vol.3, p.165: 'Neptune & four Horses – bold Sketch for a Fountain – Black chalk')

Literature: C&P: Pedretti III, 339; RL 12570

LEONARDO DA VINCI (1452-1519)

9 *Rearing horse,* 1503-05

153 x 140 mm.
Red chalk and (faded) pen and ink.

This drawing belongs to the series of studies made in preparation for Leonardo's mural painting of the *Battle of Anghiari* which he was commissioned to paint on the walls of the Salone del Cinquecento in the Palazzo Vecchio, Florence, in 1503, and which occupied him for much of the next two years. The project was abandoned in 1505, by which point only the central episode, the 'Battle for the Standard' had been painted. It was subsequently covered by Vasari's murals, and is known only through later copies.

It is clear from other preparatory studies (particularly Accademia, Venice, No.215) that both horses shown on this page were at one stage intended to frame the Standard group (to left and right), although they had disappeared by the time that the composition of this group had reached its final form. Leonardo rarely used red chalk with such verve and fluency as in the forelegs and neck of the main drawing, suggesting the shadowy form of the nude rider, and a number of alternative positions for both the horse's head and legs. The other qualities of the red chalk medium are also employed in the subtle modelling of the musculature and surface anatomy of the hind quarters.

Provenance: see under No.4

Literature: C&P; Pedretti II, 113; RL 12336

LEONARDO DA VINCI (1452-1519)

10 *Anatomical figure and action studies*
c. 1503–08

161 x 153 mm.
Red chalk with pen and ink.
Watermark: head of a bull surmounted
by a flower (fragmentary).
Compare Briquet 14950 (Ferrara, 1505)

The first drawings to be added to this sheet appear to have been the small-scale action studies lower left. These may be related to an episode in Leonardo's mural painting of the *Battle of Anghiari,* on which he was working from 1503 to 1505 (see also No.9). However, the style of the other drawing on this sheet can be related to a slightly later moment, c.1508. These drawings and notes are connected to Leonardo's study of human musculature and particularly the muscles of the shoulder. By means of these muscles the arm can be moved upwards, backwards and forwards, as shown somewhat diagramatically in the three left-hand figures, where the arm is summarily severed above the elbow. The right-hand drawing is one of a number of the standing human leg, which Leonardo examined both for its anatomy and its proportions (hence the vertical line close to the right edge of the sheet).

Leonardo's studies of human and animal anatomy were partly undertaken so that he could better represent figures in action. The juxtaposition of the two types of subject on a single sheet is therefore particularly appropriate.

Provenance: see No.4

Literature: C&P; K/P 82r; RL 12640

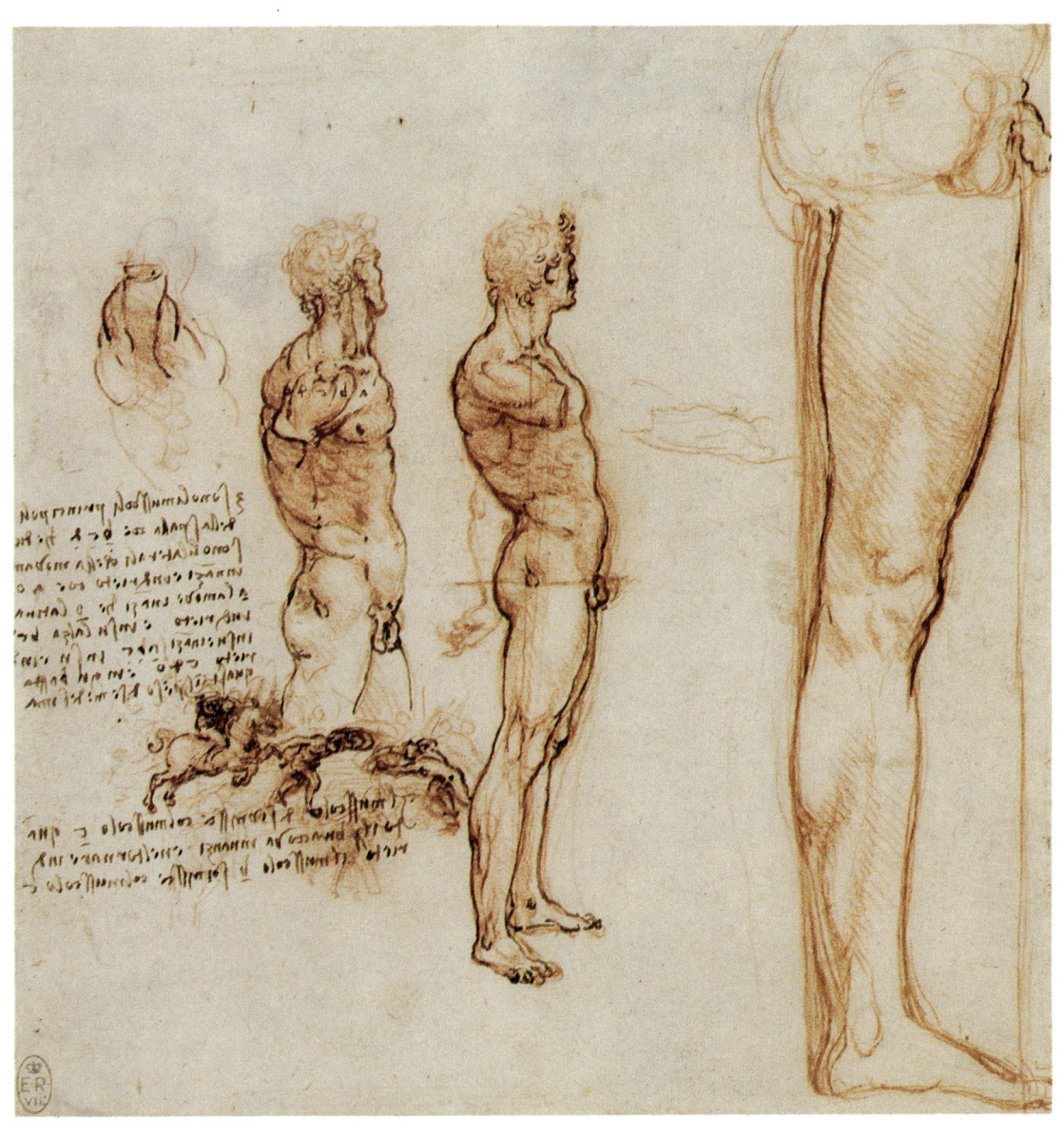

LEONARDO DA VINCI (1452-1519)

11 Studies for Leda, c.1506

198 x 166 mm (irregular).
Pen and brown ink over black chalk.
Watermark: figure (? bird) in circle (fragmentary).

The main study on this page is clearly related to the composition of *Leda*, on which Leonardo worked from c.1504 to c.1510. The proposed appearance of Leonardo's picture was recorded by Raphael in a drawing made from the older artist's cartoon (or partly finished picture?) in Florence during his stay there 1504-08 (see No.17 in this exhibition). The upper part of the body in Raphael's copy conforms in all essentials (apart from the forward gaze) to the present study. The lowered line of the right shoulder is also incorporated, rather than the partially eradicated line above and parallel to it.

Leonardo's composition is also known from a number of painted derivations, the best of which is in the Pembroke collection at Wilton House. These, and the related drawings, indicate that he continued to work on and to develop the subject over a number of years. It is possible that two cartoons of the subject were completed, one in c.1504 and the other c.1510. A picture of the standing Leda was taken by Leonardo to France at the end of his life. This was presumably the painting seen (in a ruinous state) by Cassiano dal Pozzo at Fontainebleau in 1625, of which all trace was lost by the early eighteenth century.

Leda's elaborate hairstyle, studied from front and back in two variant forms on this sheet, reflect a decorative interest which Leonardo may first have encountered in Verrocchio's studio. At the same time the coiling and interlacing lines of the hair recall the patterns observed by the artist at a similar date in both the growth of plants and the fall of water (see, for instance, RL 12424 and RL 12660). Kenneth Clark observed that 'This curious hairdress is a wig, not a plaiting of Leda's own hair', noting that Leonardo himself wrote beside one of the Leda drawings (RL 12517): 'this kind can be taken off and put on again without damaging it'. The hairstyle in No. 11 is copied line for line in the Leda painting at Wilton House.

Provenance: see under No.4 (George III, Inv. A, p.24: Leonardo, vol.1, p.21: 'two more [designs of a Lady's Head] on another Drawing, with two others of the back part of the same Head')

Literature: C&P: Pedretti III, 323; RL 12516

LEONARDO DA VINCI (1452-1519)

12   *Spray of blackberry,* c.1506/08

90 x 60 mm.
Red chalk, with touches of black chalk.

This fragment was evidently once part of a much larger sheet, from which it was cut at an early date. It belongs to a small group of studies at Windsor of *Rubus fruticosus,* with RL 12419, RL 12420 and RL 12426 (a studio work). The studies have the appearance of having been observed scientifically, from life. Leonardo may also have intended to use the drawings as subsidiary elements in a painting. The two versions of the *Virgin of the Rocks,* for instance, have dense vegetation in the foreground. The group of surviving plant studies by Leonardo are normally associated with his lost painting of *Leda and the Swan,* on which he was at work in the period c.1504 to c.1510 (see No.11). Leonardo's painting portrayed Leda as a symbol of the generative forces of nature rising amidst particularly lush vegetation. In the Richeton version of *Leda* a blackberry plant is included among the vegetation.

Provenance: see under No.4

Literature: C&P; Pedretti I, 22; RL 12425

LEONARDO DA VINCI (1452-1519)

13   *Masquerade figure*, c.1510

213 x 106 mm.
Black chalk.
Watermark: fleur de lys in coat of arms topped by cross. Compare Briquet 1571 (St Malo, 1515)

No. 13 belongs to a series of studies by Leonardo of standing figures in theatrical dress. All are drawn in black chalk on similar cream-coloured paper, of a type also found in the late drawings for the Trivulzio monument, c.1510. They must relate to a masque (or masques), performed (presumably) in Milan, Florence or Bologna, with Leonardo's assistance. He is known to have been involved in theatrical projects throughout his life.

The figure was described as a female by Clark, who compared it to a pre-Raphaelite drawing. The interlacing and loose fluttering ribbons recall the head-dress of Leda of a few years previously (see No.11). The form of the drawings in this series would suggest that they were costume designs rather than preparatory drawings for a finished painting (or print). It is surprising, therefore, that Leonardo bothered to rework the position of the right hand in his study.

Provenance: see No.4

Literature: C&P (whose reproductions transpose RL 12576 and RL 12577); Pedretti III, 355; RL 12577

FILIPPINO LIPPI (1457/8-1504)

14 *Head of a man with long hair,* c.1496

246 x 185 mm.
Metalpoint heightened with white on paper coated with a grey preparation.

Verso. Study of praying hands.
Technique as for *recto*.

The stance of the head in this drawing, together with the praying hands on the *verso* (which may be related, suggest a figure (perhaps a shepherd) in adoration. The closest relationship to be found in a finished painting appears to be with one of the shepherds behind and to the right of the Holy Family in Filippino's *Adoration of the Magi* (Florence, Uffizi), painted in 1496 for the monks of S. Donato a Scopeto. Popham recognised the study as 'An admirable original drawing of Filippino's later period'. The technique is very typical of the artist, combining rapid silverpoint drawing with white heightening, applied both in careful short hatching strokes and in broad sweeps.

Provenance: presumably George III

Literature: P&W 13; F. Ames Lewis and J. Wright, *Drawing in the Italian Renaissance Workshop,* exh. cat., Nottingham and London, 1983, No.67; RL 12822

MICHELANGELO (1475-1564)

15 *Male nude,* c.1512-1515

290 x 179 mm.
Red chalk

Verso. Male nude. Red chalk over stylus

Although Michelangelo's concern with human anatomy is well-known both from literary sources and from surviving drawings, this is one of the few pages containing evidence of his interest in human proportion. In both areas Michelangelo's work was preceded by similar studies by Leonardo da Vinci.

The unit of measurement in the present case is a head, as shown partially covered by a loosely sketched hand top right. This unit is employed to measure both the main figure (which is slightly over ten units high) and the subsidiary parts drawn to scale elsewhere on the page. Thus the knee and foot (lower left) are respectively one and one and three-quarter units, while the upper arm (top left) is two-thirds of a unit wide.

As was the case with Leonardo's proportional drawing of a horse (No.6), Michelangelo's man was evidently studied from the life, his surface anatomy carefully indicated by subtle chalk modelling. While Leonardo would have drawn the figure static and frontal, Michelangelo has chosen a pose resulting from the uneven distribution of weight, in which a strong sense of structure and balance are nevertheless retained; see, for instance, the central upright positioning of the head and neck on the straight line formed by the shoulder blades.

Stylistically this drawing is related to Michelangelo's first design for Sebastiano's *Flagellation of Christ* of the middle of the second decade, and to the later drawings for the Sistine ceiling, c.1512.

Provenance: George III
(possibly Inv.A,
p.43. Michelangelo vol.1)

Literature: P&W 421r; RL 12765

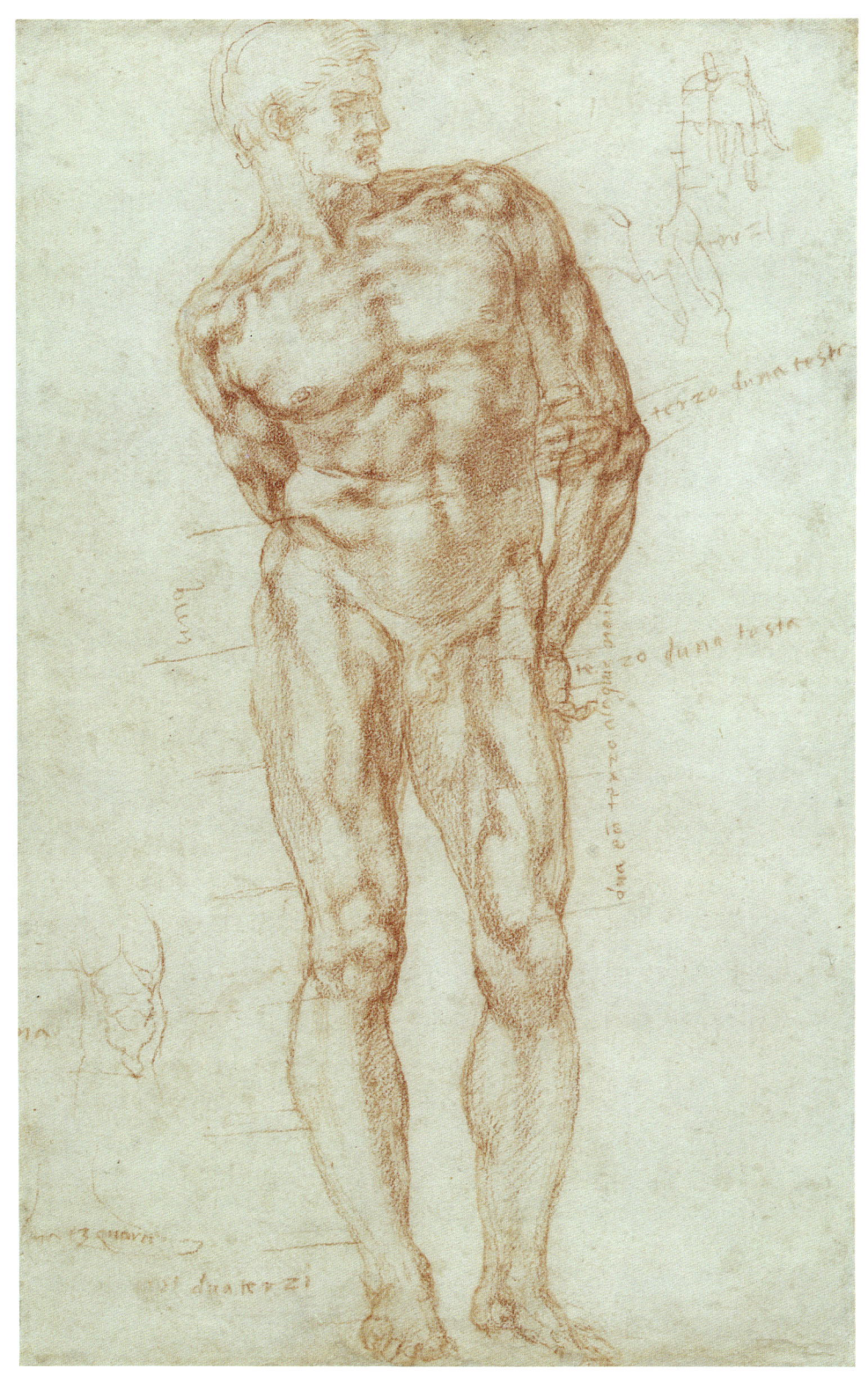

MICHELANGELO (1475-1564)

16   *Grotesque head,* c.1530/35

248 x 118 mm.
Black and red chalk.

Verso. Fragment of a recumbent male nude (after Michelangelo). Red chalk. Inscribed in black ink: *Michel Angelo Bona...* (?)

Michelangelo's combined talents as sculptor, draughtsman and painter are clearly apparent in this study of a very lively grotesque head, doubtless intended for the architectural decoration of one of his building projects. The head was first drawn and lightly shaded in red chalk, and then entirely reworked in black chalk.

The head is probably connected with Michelangelo's lengthy period of work on the Medici tombs in the New Sacristy of San Lorenzo, Florence. Compare, for instance, the decoration on the breast-plate of Duke Giuliano of the early 1530s, to which period the style of draughtsmanship would also date this drawing. Three decades later the design was reused for the giant mask in the lunette of the Porta Pia, Rome.

Provenance: George III (Inv. A, p.47. 'Michael Angelo, Fra: Bartolomeo. And: del Sarto, vol.3, p.1: A Mask Head')

Literature: P&W 425; RL 12762

RAPHAEL (1483-1520)

17 *Leda and the Swan* (after Leonardo), c. 1504-1508

310 x 190 mm.
Pen and brown ink over black chalk.
Watermark: three-peaked mountain.
Compare Briquet 11672 (omitting the cross), Udine, 1638.

Verso. Inscribed: *peze 16* (16 pieces; inverted)

The importance of the art of Leonardo in forming the mature style of Raphael has long been recognized and can be indicated very clearly in the case of the present drawing. It was evidently made by the young Raphael during his early years in Florence (1404-08), on the basis of an original work by Leonardo da Vinci, who was also resident in Florence at this time. Leonardo's lost *Leda* is discussed in detail under No. 11 above.

The drawing style and technique employed by Raphael in this copy is also reminiscent of Leonardo. The drawing was sketched in with black chalk before the final outlines were worked over in pen. The modelling was then added with a series of parallel hatching lines following the form (see also No. 11). Typically the elaborate hairstyle which must always have been present in Leonardo's Leda is shown only summarily by Raphael.

Provenance: George III (Inv. A, p.51. 'Raffaello d'Urbino e Scuola, p.37: A Leda drawn with a Pen ... immitators of Raphael's stile')

Literature: P&W 789; RL 12759

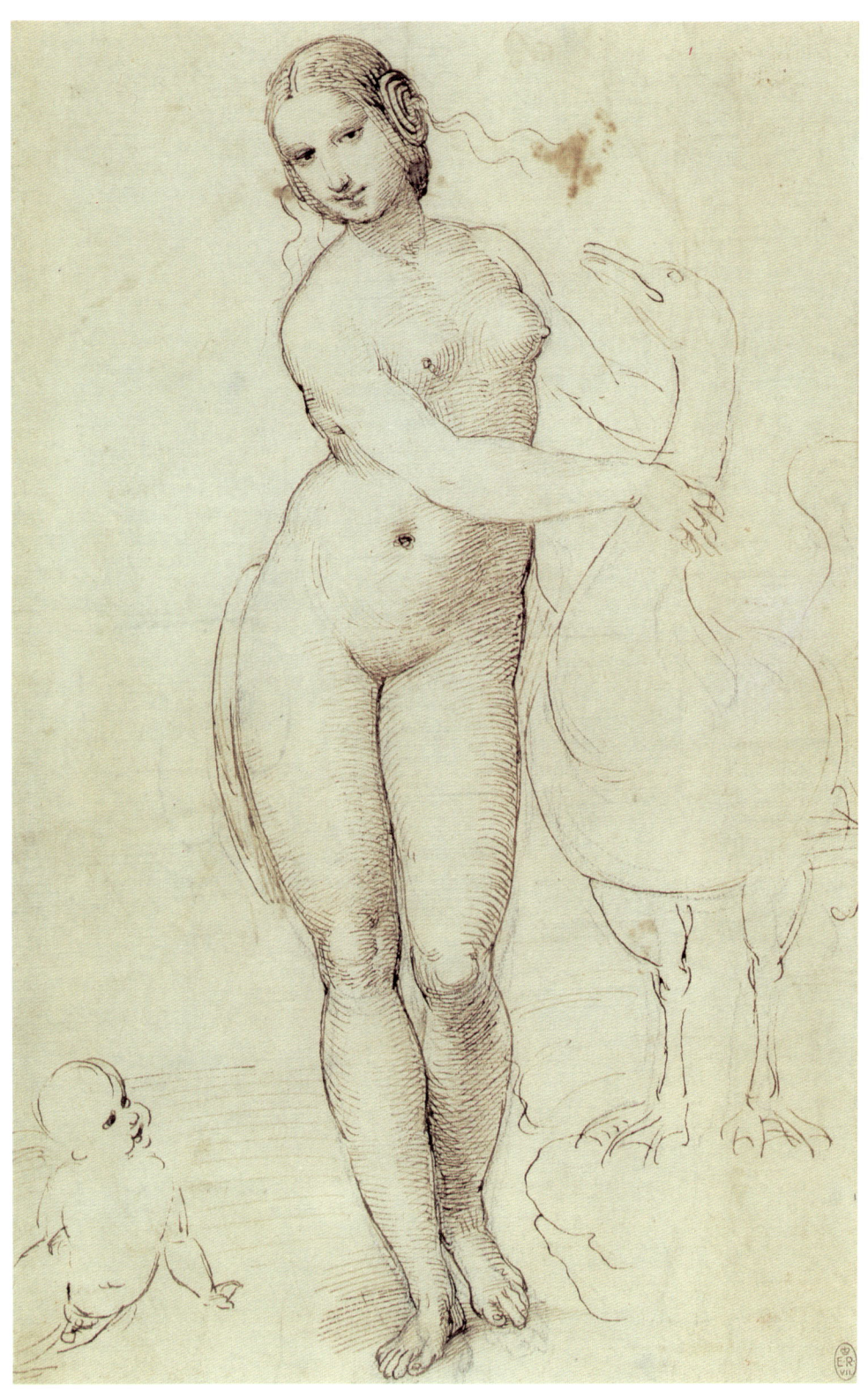

RAPHAEL (1483-1520)

18 *Nude figure with an axe,* c.1513/14

321 x 254 mm.
Black chalk on buff paper.
Watermark: crossbow within circle.
Compare Briquet 746 (Lucca, 1469-73).

Verso. Study of cattle. Pen and brown ink.

This drawing belongs to a series of figure and compositional studies which have been assembled and explained by Michael Hirst as preparatory work for an unexecuted altarpiece of the *Resurrection* for the Chigi Chapel in the Roman church of S. Maria della Pace. In 1530, ten years after the deaths of both Raphael and his patron Agostino Chigi, the commission for the same altarpiece was reassigned to Sebastiano del Piombo, who likewise failed to complete it (M. Hirst, 'The Chigi Chapel in S. Maria della Pace', *Journal of the Warburg and Courtauld Institutes,* XXIV, 1961, pp.161 ff.). Compositional studies by Raphael at Bayonne and the British Museum indicate a group of figures in the foreground shielding their eyes from the intensity of the light emanating from the supernatural visions of the Angel of the Resurrection seated on the open tomb, and of the Resurrected Christ above.

The animal studies on the *verso* are an unusual (but surely autograph) element. A connection with Raphael's preparatory work for Marcantonio's engraving of the *Morbetto,* in which various animals are included, is not impossible. A date c.1513/16 has been suggested for the engraving. A similar dating would apply for the figure study on the *recto.*

Provenance: George III (Inv. A, p.51: 'Raphaello d'Urbino e Scuola, p.33: Another soldier, [A study of part of the Groupe in the Resurrection]')

Literature: P&W 799; RL 12735

SEBASTIANO DEL PIOMBO (c.1485-1547)

19 *Holy Family with the Infant St John and a donor,* c.1530

267 x 220 mm.
Black chalk, with traces of grey paint.

Verso. Study for the infant Christ.
Black chalk with traces of white chalk, on paper coated with a blue-grey preparation. Inscribed in pen and ink: *di Fra Bart. -del piombo.*

The various studies on this sheet cannot be securely related to any one finished painting by Sebastiano. The poses (but not the respective positions) of the Virgin and St Joseph recall those in the recently rediscovered picture of the *Holy Family and St John the Baptist* in the Národní Galerie, Prague (Hirst, *op. cit.,* Pl.128), painted by Sebastiano for Pope Clement VII in 1524-25. Similar poses were reused, in reverse, for the *Madonna del Velo* in the Gallerie Nazionali at Capodimonte, Naples, in the 1530s (ibid., Pl.181). In both pictures a veil is held by the Virgin over the sleeping figure of the Christ Child. The Virgin's arms in the present drawing appear to be raised in a similar gesture, although the Christ Child is here awake, and turns away from a terrestrial globe towards the donor. The position of his arms and legs is reconsidered on the *verso* and at lower left, at which point the young St John the Baptist is also reintroduced.

The motif of the orb may be related to Parmigianino's *Madonna della Rosa* (Gemäldegalerie, Dresden) of c.1527-29, in which the Christ Child rests one arm on an orb, while holding a rose with the other.

Popham supposed that as the orb is not present in any of the preparatory drawings for Parmigianino's painting, it may have been introduced at a final stage prior to its presentation to Pope Clement VII, to typify his spiritual supremacy of the earth' (A. E. Popham, *Catalogue of the Drawings of Parmigianino,* New Haven and London, 1971, I, p.19). The head of the kneeling donor, bottom right, bears a certain resemblance to Pope Clement VII (d.1534) for whom both Sebastiano's Prague picture and Parmigianino's Dresden picture were painted.

Provenance: ? Nicholas Lanier (small 5-pointed star; Lugt 2886); George III (Inv. A, p.85. Among 'Scuola Veneziano, pp.30-34. Sebastiano del Piombo')

Literature: P&W 923; M. Hirst, *Sebastiano del Piombo,* Oxford, 1981, pp.138, 150; RL 4813

FRANCESCO SALVIATI (1510-1563)

20 *Virgin and Child with attendant Saints,* ?1540s

366 x 248 mm.
Pen and brown ink and wash, within feint black chalk and ink framing lines. Inscribed in black lead, lower left: *Francesco*.

Watermark: anchor within circle, topped by five-pointed star. Compare Briquet 495 (Prague, 1539/46)

Verso. Inscribed in pen and ink: *Francescho Saluiato.*

This study is evidently a compositional design for an altarpiece. The attribution to Salviati is surely justified, although no surviving painting by that master appears to relate to this design. Popham pointed out that 'Its arrangement indeed resembles that of the altarpiece painted by Giorgio Vasari in his youth for the Compagnia di San Rocco of Arezzo which is now in the Church of S. Sebastiano in that town'.

Provenance: presumably George III
Literature: P&W 885; RL 051

LELIO ORSI (c.1511-1587)

21   *A crossbowman,* c.1565

250 x 197 mm.
Pen and ink over black lead, with yellow and brown wash, heightened with white.
Old stain top centre.

Verso. Inscribed in brown ink: *L.X.III*

This figure of a crossbowman evidently occupied a central position in the mezzanine area of the façade of Orsi's own house in Novellara. Visitors to the house would immediately have been confronted by his uncompromisingly unwelcome attitude. The original appearance of the façade is known from drawings at Chatsworth (No.351; inscribed *al viso del vero f.*), Modena (No.1265) and Princeton (No.47-14: attribution uncertain). These show that above and to either side of the crossbowman the artist painted nudes in various positions, grappling both with each other and with two collapsing flaming columns. In the upper centre reclining nudes resting on clouds supported the artist's coat of arms of two bears ('orsi') drinking from a fountain. The sharp foreshortening of this single figure is explained by the elevated position that it was to occupy.

Orsi's work on house façades in Novellara is related to an order issued by Alfonso Gonzaga in September 1563 for all the house façades of Novellara to be painted. Characteristically the figure shows the joint influences of Correggio and Guilio Romano.

Provenance: George III (Inv.A, p.85. 'Scuola Veneziano, pp.12-14: Paolo Cagliari detto Paolo Veronese'. Identification through numbering)

Literature: P&W 529; RL 4791

ALBRECHT DÜRER (1471-1528)

22 'Pupila Augusta', c.1490

254 x 194 mm.
Pen and black ink, with additions in brown ink. Signed with monogram (in reverse), and dated (not by the artist) 1516.
The scroll lower right inscribed (in reverse): PVPILA. AVGVSTA

Watermark: crown topped by cross (fragmentary). Compare Briquet 4804 (Venice, 1491-2 etc.)

For an explanation of both its meaning and its content this drawing has occupied generations of scholars. In summary, 'The drawing, planned as the model for an engraving, ... is an early example of humanist influence on a northern artist and shows Dürer's veneration for the art of the Italian Renaissance. It was made about 1500 in Nuremberg' (Schilling catalogue).

'Pupila augusta', translated as 'august ward', refers to the youthful Venus, conveyed (with her two companions) by a dolphin towards her protectors, the Three Graces, in the foreground. The drawing is an eclectic assemblage of types and forms collected by the artist during his first twenty years. The buildings in the background (which reappear in the engraving of *St Anthony*) are taken from Dürer's view of the valley of Trent, to which single buildings from his watercolour of Innsbruck are added. The figures were taken from a variety of Italian sources, carefully studied and integrated by Dürer shortly after his first visit to Italy.

It has been suggested that the reason that Dürer failed to complete either this drawing or the intended engraving was a belated realisation that although the monogram and inscription were reversed, for eventual printed reproduction in mirror-image, the foreground figures had each been shown right-handed in the drawing, rather than left-handed as they should have been.

Provenance: George III (Inv. A, p.15. 'Albert Dürer e Maestri Antichi Div:si, p.52 [addition?]: an allegorical subject found amongst the Prints — Albert Dürer')

Literature: S 23; RL 12175

ALBRECHT DÜRER (1471–1528)

23 *Virgin and Child with a musical angel*, 1519

304 x 213 mm.
Pen and black ink, with additions in brown ink. Signed with monogram (fragmentary) and dated *1519* along lower edge.

This drawing was described by Schilling as 'among the most beautiful Madonnas in Dürer's new Italian mood'. The influence of Italian (and specifically Venetian) art can be felt in the triangular form of the draped figure of the Virgin, seated against a hanging backcloth in an open landscape, and in the musical angel at her feet. Both elements had first appeared in Dürer's *Feast of the Rose Garlands*, painted over ten years earlier, in 1506. Typically northern elements are the angular terminations of the drapery folds, the use of nobbly tree stumps (rather than classical architectural elements) to support the Virgin's throne, and the ink colour and texture.

The artist has worked over a number of small areas in brown ink. No more finished composition (painting, woodcut or engraving) related to this drawing appears to have survived. It may therefore have been intended as an independent work of art, in which case the inclusion of the 'construction line' below the Virgin's nose is somewhat surprising.

Provenance: George III (Inv. A, p.15. 'Albert Dürer e Maestri Antichi Div:si, p.23: Virgin Mary Child & Angel playing on a violin. 1519 AD')

Literature: S 22; RL 12180

HANS HOLBEIN THE YOUNGER (1497/8-1543)

24 *Sir Thomas Strange,* 1536

243 x 209 mm.
Black, white and coloured chalks
on pink prepared paper.
Inscribed in gold and red, top left:
Tho: Strange. Knight

Sir Thomas Strange (or Lestrange) of Hunstanton (1494–1545) was a loyal servant of the Crown during the Dissolution of the Monasteries and was Sheriff of Norfolk from 1532. Earlier he served as Esquire to the Body to Henry VIII and was present at the Field of the Cloth of Gold in 1520. He was knighted in 1529. His wife was the sister of the poet Thomas, Lord Vaux, who was also portrayed by Holbein (PH 24 and 30).

This sensitive drawing was the preparatory study for Holbein's oil painting of Thomas Strange, now in the Kimbell Museum, Fort Worth, which bears a later or retouched inscription:
ANNO De 1536 . . . Æ TATIS SVÆ 43.
(see J. Rowlands, *Holbein,* Oxford, 1985, No.59, p.143 and pl.95). In the painting, which passed by descent through the sitter's family until the start of this century, the head (and particularly the eyes) are turned more towards the spectator. Sir Thomas seems somewhat older, and is more heavily bearded, in the painting.

Provenance: from the 'great booke' of Holbein's drawings, owned successively by Edward VI (d.1553); Henry FitzAlan, Earl of Arundel (d.1580); Lord Lumley (d.1609); Henry, Prince of Wales (d.1612); Charles I; between 1627 and 1639 exchanged with the Earl of Pembroke and given by him to Thomas Howard, Earl of Arundel (d.1646); in the Royal Collection again by 1675; noted in the Kensington Inventory, 1727; the 'great booke' was broken up 1727/8, the contents framed and glazed for hanging at Richmond Lodge and then Kensington Palace; King George III (Inv.A, p.57. Holbein, vol.2, p.11: Sir Thomas Strange)

Literature: PH 43; RL 12244

HANS HOLBEIN THE YOUNGER (1497/8-1543)

25 *Lady Lister,* c.1540

289 x 208 mm.
Pen and black ink, with black and coloured chalks on pink prepared paper. Inscribed along upper edge, in gold and red: *The Lady Lister.*

Watermark: two-handled vase with single-flowered cresting. Compare Briquet 12863 (The Hague, 1524)

The sitter was possibly the wife of Sir Richard Lister (d.1552), Attorney-General, Chief Baron of the Exchequer and (from 1546) Lord Chief Justice. Alternatively, the portrait could represent one of the two wives of Sir Richard's son, Michael, who was knighted in 1537.

No related oil painting is known, but from the token inclusion of decorative detail (such as the jewelled flowers on the gable-end of Lady Lister's hood, and her necklace) this drawing cannot have been considered a finished work of art in its own right. It dates from Holbein's second English period, probably c.1540. The head-dress type recurs in a number of the artist's English portraits and is explained in the British Museum drawing of two views of a standing English gentlewoman (1895-9-15-991). One end of the hood is flicked up over the gable peak, while the other end (seen in outline over Lady Lister's left shoulder) remains hanging down.

The status of the pen and ink drawing in Holbein's work has been the subject of much discussion, the cruder lines often being attributed to a later retoucher. The pitfalls involved in value judgements of this type are clearly shown in the present portrait, where the crude ink work of the decorated gable of Lady Lister's head-dress is clearly autograph, as is the much more delicate drawing of her eyebrows.

Provenance: see under No.24
(Inv.A, p.58. Holbein, vol.2, p.24: Lady Lister)

Literature: PH 20; RL 12219

HANS HOLBEIN THE YOUNGER (1497/8-1543)

26 *John Poyntz,* c.1540

295 x 233 mm.
Pen and black ink with coloured chalks on pink prepared paper. Inscribed top left in gold and red: *John Poines.*
Watermark: hand topped by five-pointed star. Compare Briquet 11369 (Utrecht, 1541).

The inscriptions on the Windsor Holbein series were apparently copied from those added to the 'great booke' by Sir John Cheke, Edward VI's tutor and secretary. That on the present drawing identifies the sitter with one of the two gentlemen by the name of John Poyntz at the court of Henry VIII. A closely related oil painting at Sandon Hall bears the arms of John Poyntz of Alderley, Gloucestershire, who must therefore be the sitter represented in this drawing (see J. Rowlands, *op. cit.* in No.24, under R.24, p.233). He was the son of Sir Robert Poyntz of Iron Acton, and the uncle of Sir Nicholas Poyntz, the subject of another of Holbein's drawings at Windsor (PH 34). John Poyntz's first wife, Elizabeth, was a sister of Sir Henry Guildford (d.1532), successively Master of the Horse, Comptroller of the Household and Chamberlain of the Exchequer to Henry VIII (see PH 10). John Poyntz of Alderley died in November 1544, after accompanying the King to fight in France earlier in the year.

The oil painting at Sandon gives the sitter's age as 41 and shows the altered line of the sitter's back, running vertically within the bulkier contour first suggested in the drawing. It includes a parapet along the bottom of the picture.

Provenance: see under No.24
(Inv. A, p.57. Holbein, vol.2, p.9: John Poines)

Literature: PH 54; RL 12233

AUGUSTIN HIRSCHVOGEL (1503-1553)

27 *The Crucifixion*, 1533

568 x 400 mm.
Pen and black ink over traces of black lead within old black ink border. Dated bottom right: *1533*. Inscribed bottom right with forged Cranach monogram: *LC*.

Watermark: crowned double-headed eagle, with tailpiece. Compare Briquet 1457 (Utrecht, 1519-21)

Verso. Inscribed in ink: *D..26: Aug...1674*

No. 27 presents an unusual (and perspectivally rather uncertain) view of Golgotha, situated (according to medieval illustrative tradition) outside the walls of a northern town. The main participants are encircled by a vast crowd of onlookers.

The date (1533) inscribed on No. 27 has allowed it to be used as one of the main reference points in the recreation of Hirschvogel's graphic style. This drawing is securely placed within the artist's early years (until 1536) in Nuremberg. Augustin Hirschvogel is not known to have painted any pictures (although he was active as a stained glass painter). The finished form of the present drawing suggests that it may have been destined for a patron.

The watermark is a variant of one recorded by Briquet. However it is virtually identical to that found in a group of Holbein drawings at Windsor, which includes the preparatory study for the portrait of Sir Richard Southwell, dated 1536 (PH 35). See J. Roberts, *Drawings by Holbein from the Court of Henry VIII*, exh. cat., Houston, 1987, pp. 142-3, Type D.

Provenance: George III (Inv. A, p.14. 'Albert Dürer e Maestri Antichi Div:si, pp.11-14: A Crucifix in the early age of the rise of Painting')

Literature: S 31; J. S. Peters, 'Early drawings by A. Hirschvogel', *Master Drawings*, XXVII, No.4, 1979, p.392, No.63; RL 12172

LUDOVICO CARRACCI (1555-1619)

28 Saints and angels in adoration, c.1605

456 x 206 mm.
Pen and ink and brown wash over black chalk with the white heightening on cream paper with a buff wash. Squared for transfer with an old horizontal fold across the centre. A drawing by Parmigianino of a girl holding a crucifix (198 x 100 mm. Pen and brown ink and brown wash with white heightening) is inlaid into the upper part of the sheet.

Verso. Inscribed in brown ink: . . . *esto ed il disegno che* . . . *restati d'acc* . . . / . . . *sosteuole de* . . . / *Io Alles.ro Barb* . . .

The squaring of Ludovico's drawing would seem to suggest that it was made with the express purpose of transfer to a larger scale. However no such related work is known. The page was evidently kept folded across the middle for some time. Parmigianino's study does not appear to have been folded and its connection with the larger sheet cannot therefore have been envisaged when Ludovico made his drawing. In addition, the inscription on the *verso* of Ludovico's drawing was cut when Parmigianino's fragment was inserted. Either the Windsor Parmigianino drawing or a damaged version of it in the Louvre (inv. 6490) was reproduced (in reverse) in an etching by Guido Reni (Bartsch XVIII, p. 302, No. 49), presumably made during Reni's early years in Bologna. It is possible that the inscription on the *verso* refers to Reni's friend Alessandro Barbieri (see Malvasia, *Felsina Pittrice*, 1841 ed., II, pp. 33, 47, 51 and 52).

Wittkower considered that 'the monumentality of the figures [in Ludovico's drawing] would seem to suggest a date in the mid-1590s, the period of the *Transfiguration* in the Pinacoteca, Bologna, but the style of draughtsmanship is later, probably not before 1605' (Wittkower catalogue).

Provenance: [Allessandro Barbieri]; Bonfiglioli collection (1719 Richardson; not mentioned in 1696 inv.); Zaccaria Sagredo; Consul Joseph Smith; 1762 purchased for George III (Inv.A, p. 77. Carracci, vol. 11. Identification by numbering)

Literature: W 46; RL 2336

ANNIBALE CARRACCI (1560-1609)

29 Studies for two of Perseus' warriors, c.1603/04

334 x 237 mm.
Black and white chalk on blue paper.

This study is a preliminary study for two of the figures in the left background of Annibale's fresco of *Perseus and Phineus* in the Gallery of the Palazzo Farnese, Rome (see D. Posner, *Annibale Carracci*, London, 1971, Plate 140d). After completing the decoration of the ceiling of the Gallery in 1600, Annibale began work on the walls below c.1603/04. It is generally thought that only the *Perseus and Phineus* composition was entirely Annibale's work. Other areas of the mural decoration were entrusted to his assistants, particularly Domenichino and Lanfranco.

The subjects of the wall paintings were taken from Greek mythology (specifically Ovid's *Metamorphoses*, Book V). Perseus, the son of Zeus and Danae, turned to stone his rival for the love of Andromeda, Phineus, by showing him the head of Medusa. The figures in this drawing shield their faces from the scene, lest they be similarly transformed. According to the late seventeenth-century biographer, Bellori, the subject represented the victory of virtue over vice.

Provenance: George III
(Inv.A, p.76. Carracci, vol.6.
Identification by numbering)

Literature: W 297; RL 2072

GUIDO RENI (1575-1642)

30 *Samson slaying the Philistines*, 1607/08

367 x 200 mm.
Pen and ink and brown wash
over black chalk in old ink framing lines.
Watermark: bird within circle.
Compare Briquet 12204 (Naples, 1494)

Verso. Figure study of Samson.
Black chalk.

Contrary to the eighteenth-century description in Inventory A, this drawing is related to the upright format of the fresco in the Sala delle Nozze Aldobrandini in the Vatican Palace (of 1607-08) rather than to the later oil painting, of irregular but broader proportions, now in the Pinacoteca Nazionale, Bologna (1618-19; see S. Pepper, *Guido Reni,* Oxford, 1984, cat. nos. 29 and 60; Plates 32 and 86). The fresco was one of a series representing the Feats of Samson, painted by Reni for Cardinal Scipione Borghese, in the room which served as his antechamber. The other subjects represented (taken from Judges XIV-XVI) were the killing of the lion and the removal of the gates of Gaza. The present drawing shows how Samson 'found the jaw-bone of an ass, all raw, and picked it up and slew a thousand men' (Judges XV, 15). In the finished fresco the composition is simplified to include Samson and only two or three opponents.

Provenance: Bonfiglioli Collection (1696 Inv., p.12, 1.3: 'Un Dissegno Istoria di Sansone che ammazza i filistei mano di Guido in Cornice, e cassetta dorata con vetro'); Zaccaria Sagredo; Consul Joseph Smith; 1762 purchased for George III (Inv. A, p.80. Guido &c, vol.5, p.1: 'A first study for his Sampson destroying the Philistines; Painted at Bologna in the Palazzo Publico')

Literature: BM 383; V. Birke, *Guido Reni: Zeichnungen,* exh. cat., Vienna, Albertina, 1981, No. 20; RL 3410

GUERCINO (1591-1666)

31 *The Annunciation,* c.1616

220 x 174 mm.
Pen and ink with wash.

The angel descends on a cloud, carrying a lily, to announce the forthcoming birth of Christ to the Virgin Mary. The subject suggests that the design may have been intended for a small devotional picture, but no such related work is known.

The angel appears originally to have been holding a burning torch. His pose is closely related (in reverse) to that of Prometheus in the painting of *Prometheus bringing the statue of clay to life with a burning torch* (Cassa di Risparmio, Cento), painted by Guercino in 1616 on the chimney-breast of one of the rooms of his Accademia in Cento. An early date, around that time, is therefore indicated for this drawing.

Provenance: George III (Inv.A,p.66. Guercino, vol.9: 'A Salutation')

Literature: M&T139; RL 2792

GUERCINO (1591-1666)

32 *Two helmeted soldiers on horseback,*
c. 1615/30

343 x 231 mm.
Pen and brown ink

This drawing appears to be a study for part of a larger composition, presumably relating to a battle scene. The figure seen in back view holds a marshal's baton, while that facing us at the right holds a standard. A group of archers are poised to release their bow-strings and arrows, bottom left.

No directly related painting is known, but there is a general resemblance with Guercino's frescoes in the Casa Provenzale, Cento, dated c. 1614. Although No. 32 may be attributable to this early period, a dating c. 1630 has also been proposed.

Provenance: George III (Inv. A, p.60. Guercino, vol. 1: 'Soldiers & Horsemen')

Literature: M&T 169; RL 2397

CARLO MARATTA (1625-1713)

33 *Allegory in honour of Pietro da Cortona*, c.1674

415 x 301 mm.
Black chalk.
Watermark: Fleur de lys within double circle topped by a letter 'V'. Compare Heawood 1591 (Venice, 1690)

Verso. Study for the seated figure of Time, holding a blank tablet. Black chalk.

The seated figure of winged Father Time holds a portrait medallion while trampling underfoot a fallen man, the personification of Envy. The Portrait agrees in all essentials with that of the Italian painter and architect, Pietro da Cortona (1596-1669), in a medal by François Chéron. The identification is also supplied in Mariette's entry for Francesco Bartolozzi's engraving after this drawing, in his list of prints after Maratta's works.

Chéron's medal was presumably made during his stay in Rome between 1669 (the year of Pietro da Cortona's death) and 1675. It was itself based on a portrait by Ciro Ferri, but the medallion in No. 32 appears to depend on the work of Chéron rather than on Ferri's original. It is possible that Maratta's drawing was commissioned at the same time, c.1674. No. 32 is apparently *en suite* with another commemorative drawing by Maratta, also in the Royal Collection. The second drawing, which was also engraved by Bartolozzi, was made in honour of Claude Lorrain (BR 318). It is in a slightly different style to No.32, and was probably executed somewhat later, following Claude's death in 1682.

Provenance: Pope Clement XI; Albany family; 1762 purchased for George III (Inv. A, p.107. Carlo Maratta, vol. 1: among 'Two designs for Monuments, Engrav'd by F. Bartolozi')

Literature: BR 317; BM, p.97; J.K. and R.H. Westin, *Carlo Maratti and his contemporaries*, exh. cat., Philadelphia, 1975, No. 21; RL 4091.

GIOVANNI BENEDETTO CASTIGLIONE (1610-1663/5)

34 *'Omnia Vanitas'*, c.1650

391 x 542 mm.
Drawn in brown oil paint (various shades).
Inscribed in pencil top right: *10.*

Both in subject-matter and in content this drawing is closely related to Castiglione's oil painting in the Nelson-Atkins Museum of Art, Kansas City (ill. Percy, op. cit., Fig. 16). That picture is dated to the artist's second stay in Rome, c.1650. At around the same time Castiglione was producing a large number of drawings in this very particular brush and oil technique, which doubtless owed something to the example of the oil sketches of Rubens and Van Dyck.

The composition of No.34 is tighter than that in the related oil and did not necessarily precede it. In both, the short-lived delights of music, dance, theatre, the hunt, and so on, are carefully depicted, as symbols of vanity.

Provenance: Zaccaria Sagredo; Consul Joseph Smith; 1762 purchased for George III (Inv.A, p.131. Castiglione, vol.V 'Of Large Drawings': 'Musick & a Woman dancing')

Literature: BC 134; A. Percy, *G.B. Castiglione*, exh. cat., Philadelphia, 1971, No.40; RL 4050

NICOLAS POUSSIN (1594-1665)

35 *The Origin of Coral*, c.1626/7

226 x 312 mm.
Pen and ink and brown wash over red chalk on oatmeal-textured paper, in old (fragmentary) framing lines.

Like the composition for which the figures in No.29 were drawn, this study relates to the adventures of Perseus, as recounted in Ovid's *Metamorphoses*, Book IV. Perseus has freed Andromeda (seated centre left) by killing the sea monster Medusa and now washes the Gorgon's blood from his arms. But just as Medusa's face turned men to stone when they looked at her, so her head resting on the ground behind Perseus transforms the plants on which blood falls into coral. This particular subject is only rarely encountered, but Cardinal Massimi (to whom No.35 once belonged) commissioned a painting of the same scene from Claude (1674; Viscount Coke collection).

'The Origin of Coral' was probably drawn as one of the group of three, with 'The Kingdom of Flora', and 'Venus and Adonis hunting' during Poussin's early years in Rome, c.1626/27.

Provenance: Cardinal Massimi (Massimi catalogue, p.13, No.23: 'Perseo ed Andromeda'); Dr Richard Mead; Frederick, Prince of Wales; George III (Inv.A, p.98. 'N. Poussin. The Smaller Volume, page 23: Sacrifice to [Priapus]')

Literature: BF 170; RL 11984

NICOLAS POUSSIN (1594-1665)

36 *The death of Virginia*, c.1635

177 x 233 mm.
Pen and brown ink and brown wash, within ink framing lines.
Watermark: bird on orb within circle.
Unrecorded.

Verso. Bacchus and Ariadne.
Pen and brown ink.

One of a number of subjects from Roman history, drawn by Poussin in the 1630s, No. 36 shows in the centre foreground the death of the centurion's daughter, Virginia, at the hand of her father who is seen rushing away, knife in hand, towards the right. One of the decemvirs, Appius Claudius, had become enamoured of Virginia and had her claimed as a slave in order to obtain possession of her. Her father killed Virginia to protect her honour.

This drawing has been described as among Poussin's most brilliant virtuoso performances as a draughtsman', in which 'the simple but expressive outline is combined with an exceptionally luminous use of wash, the effect of which is made more striking, by the ... immaculate state of preservation' (A. Blunt, *The Drawings of Poussin*, New Haven and London, 1979, pp.41 and 43). It is normally dated c.1635.

Provenance: Albani collection; 1762 purchased for George III (Inv.A, p.101. 'N. Poussin. The Larger Volume, page 14: Virginius slays his Daughter to save her honour from the Tyrant Decembir Appius')

Literature: BF 193r; RL 11888r

NICOLAS POUSSIN (1594-1665)

37 *The Agony in the Garden,* c.1637

285 x 241 mm
(two irregular conjoined sheets
linked by a 5 mm deep horizontal strip).
Pen and ink and brown wash on blue paper.

Watermark: sacred monogram (IHS) topped by cross within an oval. Compare Briquet 2976 (Mayence, n.d.).

This drawing was evidently cut in two at an early stage; the lower part itself has three old tears which have now been patched. The 5 mm horizontal strip across the lower part of the drawing has been inserted and touched in to visually unite the composition.

As was often the case, Poussin rethought the traditional iconography of the Agony in the Garden, depicting Christ lying prone (rather than kneeling) on the hilltop, his praying hands in front of the kneeling figures of an angel and of Ecclesia (a personification of the Church). Three sleeping disciples are shown in the foreground. The scene is dramatically lit by a supernatural light which obscures facial features of all the protagonists.

The composition may be related to a painting of the same subject described by Sandrart in the collection of Poussin's patron Cassiano dal Pozzo. The drawing is generally dated c.1637.

Provenance: LOWER PART: Cardinal Massimi (Massimi catalogue, p.35 No.59: 'Li Discepoli nell' Horto'); Dr Richard Mead; Frederick, Prince of Wales; George III (Inv.A, p.100. 'N Poussin. The Smaller Volume, page 59: The Three Disciples a Sleep in the Garden')
UPPER PART: Cardinal Albani; 1762 purchased for George III (Inv.A, p.101. 'N. Poussin. The Larger Volume, page 1: . . . Abraham adoring God accompany'd by two Angels')

Literature: BF 196; RL 051

CLAUDE LORRAIN (1600-1682)

38 *The 'Campo Vaccino'*, c.1630

127 x 92 mm.
Pen and ink with wash.
Fragmentary old framing line.

The 'Campo Vaccino' or 'cow plain', was the name by which the Roman Forum was described during the seventeenth century while cattle were allowed to graze there. On the left in this drawing is Vignola's gateway (now destroyed) to the Farnese Gardens on the Palatine Hill, while in the background is the Church of S. Maria Liberatrice, remodelled by Onorio Longhi in 1617 but destroyed in 1900 to reveal the remains of the church of S. Maria Antiqua beneath it.

Claude's seventeenth-century biographer Baldinucci stated that 'he took no displeasure in having figures in his landscapes or sea pieces added by another hand'. The quality of the figure drawing in the present sheet is markedly inferior to that of Claude's contemporary Poussin, for instance.

The oil stain in the sky of No.38 could have occurred during the tracing process preparatory for George Lewis's engraving of 1809 (published in J. Chamberlaine, *Original Designs . . . in his Majesty's Collection*, London, 1812, Pl.44). That print was among those copied by John Constable (I. Fleming-Williams, *Constable, Landscape Watercolours and Drawings*, London, 1976, p.90 and note 6).

See also No. 39.

Provenance: [?Cardinal Massimi;] George III (Inv.A, p.115.'Paesi di Claudio Loranese e altri, [among] Eight Landscapes mostly large Drawings of Claudio Loranese, Seventeen small studies - ten pages')

Literature: BF51; H. Diane Russell, *Claude Lorrain,* exh.cat., Washington, 1982-83, No.Dl; RL 13085

Claude Lorrain (1600-1682)

39 *An artist drawing,* c.1630

127 x 93 mm.
Pen and ink (numerous old repairs).
Fragmentary old framing line.

The subject of this drawing - an artist sketching a piece of sculpture (scarcely visible in its architectural niche) in an open landscape - was particularly appropriate both to the artist and to the moment, Rome in the 1620s/30s. These were the years in which Cassiano dal Pozzo's artists (who included Poussin and Pietro Testa) were making their drawings of classical antiquities for his 'museo cartacei', which today survives, largely intact, scattered between the Royal Library, the British Museum and a number of other collections. Claude was not involved in this project, but certainly knew of its existence.

Nos. 38 and 39 belong to a group of 38 small drawings by Claude which may once have made up a single notebook. Twelve of these drawings are in the Royal Collection, while others are in the British Museum and elsewhere. Several incorporate views of buildings in and around Rome, which was Claude's home from 1625 until his death in 1682. Joachim von Sandrart, who was in Rome from 1628 to 1635, records many drawing and painting expeditions to the Roman Campagna with Claude.

Provenance: see under No.38

Literature: BF 59; H. Diane Russell, op. cit., No.D4; RL 13092

CLAUDE LORRAIN (1600-1682)

40 *The Temple of Apollo at Delphi,* 1672

254 x 318 mm.
Pen and ink, black lead and grey wash with white heightening. Signed and dated bottom left: *Claud[e] IVF / Roma. 1672 / Rom.*

Inscribed: *Il tempio di Apollo in Delfo sopral' monte pe . . . / cauata da giustino historico*

As Claude himself noted in the inscription, this drawing shows the Temple of Apollo on Mount Parnassus, as described in Marcus Justinus, *Historiae Philippicae*, a work which was at the time available in both Italian and French translation. In the foreground a group of figures and animals proceed along the route to the mountain, in order to make their sacrifice.

The drawing is related to Claude's oil painting of the same subject in the Art Institute of Chicago (H. Diane Russell, *op. cit.,* No. P50). This and its pendant *(Perseus and the Origin of Coral)* were painted for Cardinal Massimi in 1683. There are a number of variations between drawing and painting, chief of which is an increased sense of space between the tree on the right and the mountain, an effect which is also assisted by the elimination of the hillock in the foreground.

Diane Russell has suggested that the initials following Claude's signature may stand for 'Invenit et fecit', indicating that the artist was responsible both for the original concept and for the execution of the drawing. He used the same abbreviations in the drawn copies he made of his own work, and in his etchings.

Provenance: see under No. 38

Literature: BF 47; H. Diane Russell, *op. cit.,* No. D68; RL 13079

CANALETTO (1697-1768)

41 *St Paul's and the City of London seen through an arch of Westminster Bridge,* 1746

289 x 485 mm.
Pen and ink and grey wash over traces of pencil within a ruled ink framing line.

When Canaletto first arrived in London in May 1746 he would have found the new Westminster Bridge in an advanced state of completion. It was finally opened five months later. This drawing, and a closely related one in the Albright Art Gallery, Buffalo, are connected to a painting of the same subject commissioned by Sir Hugh Smithson before 1747, when an engraving of it by Remigius Parr was published. The painting is still in the collection of the Duke of Northumberland.

Westminster Bridge was the first new bridge to be built over the Thames in London for over six hundred years, and was naturally a subject of great interest to Londoners and tourists alike. Canaletto's views appear to have had an instant appeal for the British artist, Samuel Scott (1702-72). The wide span of the bridge was treated in the same way as the arch of a classical ruin, through which vistas were observed in many of Canaletto's 'capricci'. It has recently been suggested that the inspiration for such arched vistas was a painting by the Italian artist Antonio Jolli at Richmond House, London. It was described as an 'arched piece of building through which the view of St. George's Church & ye Custom house in Venice are seen'. Jolli was active in London between 1744 and 1748.

Charles Lennox, 2nd Duke of Richmond, was also a patron of Canaletto (see Francis Russell's entry for No.157 in *The Treasure Houses of Britain*, ed. G. Jackson-Stops, exh. cat., Washington, 1985-6).

Provenance: Consul Joseph Smith; 1762 purchased for George III (Inv. A, p.116: among 139 drawings by Canaletto: The Drawings are the Studys of the great Collection of his paintings bought by His Majesty of Mr Smith of Venice')

Literature: PC119; C/L 732; RL 7561

CANALETTO (1697-1768)

42   *The Piazza S. Marco, Venice,
with S. Geminiano*, c.1756

193 x 269 mm.
Pen and brown ink with grey wash over traces of pencil within black ink framing lines.

Nos. 42 and 43 may have been drawn as companion pieces. The confident and slick draughtsmanship together with the masterly addition of wash, has suggested a dating soon after Canaletto's final return from England in 1755. The drawings give a brilliant indication both of the life and of the light in the Piazza S. Marco which was the central meeting place of Venice in the eighteenth century, as today. The architecture is indicated with a tight control of detail and perspective so that we think we see everything, whereas in fact we are only shown a part and that part is somewhat distorted.

In No. 42 our viewpoint is from the Procuratie Nuove, looking towards the Procuratie Vecchie (on the right) and the asymmetrically-placed façade of S. Geminiano to left of centre.

Provenance: see under No. 41

Literature: PC 56; C/L 529; RL 7433

CANALETTO (1697-1768)

43 *The Piazza S. Marco, Venice, looking towards S. Marco,* c.1756

198 x 281 mm (irregular).
Pen and dark brown ink with grey wash over traces of pencil within black ink framing lines.

The viewpoint in No.43 is taken from the same arcade as in No.42, but now looking north-west towards the façade of S. Marco and the Torre del Orologio. The view may depend in part on Canaletto's early sketch on f. 8r of his Quaderno in the Accademia, Venice. The extra storey that was added to the Torre del Orologio between 1755 and 1757 is not shown, suggesting that the view must have been drawn very soon after Canaletto's return from England in 1755. The fact that the Campanile was at first drawn further to the left (hence the vertical pentimento) suggests that No.43 must be the first in the group of closely related works of this subject, leading up to the small upright oil in the National Gallery, London (No. 2516).

The figures in the right foreground are gathered outside the Café Florian, which occupies the same premises today as it did in Canaletto's time. To achieve the double vista down the arcade of the Procuratie Nuove and out across the Piazza, Canaletto has used his customary artistic licence; the wide columns and narrow bays of the arcade make such a double vista impossible in reality.

Provenance: see under No. 41

Literature: PC 57; C/L 525; RL 7427

GIOVANNI BATTISTA PIAZZETTA (1683-1754)

44   *The Procuress,* c. 1735/40

406 x 555 mm
Black and white chalk on
discoloured grey-brown paper.

The thirty-six drawings by Piazzetta in the Royal Collection arrived there, in frames, within a decade of the artist's death. The drawings are uniform in type, showing between one and three figures, half-length, drawn in black and white chalks on paper which was originally blue but has now faded to grey-brown (through prolonged exposure to light). Several of the drawings (including No.44) were engraved by G.Cattini for the *Icones and vivum expressae*, first published in 1743, which further increased the popularity of this type of subject.

In No.44 Piazzetta has assembled three heads which were first studied independently in other drawings. The old woman on the right is probably first seen in a drawing in Dresden of c.1735-38, while the 'bravo' appears in a drawing in Chicago (see G.Knox, *Piazzetta*, exh. cat., Washington 1983-84, No.47).

Provenance: Consul Joseph Smith; 1762 purchased for George III (framed as pictures, so not mentioned in Inventory A)

Literature: BV 32; RL01251

PAUL SANDBY (c.1730-1809)

45 *View of the Lower Ward, Windsor Castle, from the foot of the Round Tower,* c.1765

285 x 610 mm.
Pen and black ink and watercolour over pencil, in black ink framing line.

This view of the Lower Ward is perhaps Paul Sandby's masterpiece. Hesitation arises only because the brilliant miniaturist handling of the architecture is more usually associated with the military topography and the panoramas of Paul's brother, Thomas Sandby. The respective responsibilities of the two brothers for the 'classic' Windsor views of the 1760s will probably never be satisfactorily elucidated.

The view westwards down the Lower Ward is surprisingly unchanged today, after over two hundred years. No.48 shows an intermediate stage, looking up eastwards to the viewpoint of No.45. Already by that time the avenues of small trees along the south side of St George's and in front of the Guard Room had been removed. The early nineteenth-century remodelling of the castle also 'mediaevalised' the west end of the Lower Ward (centre middle distance) and the red brick buildings in the right foreground. In Sandby's time these buildings included a refreshment area, indicated by the tiny inscription 'Coffie and Tea' above the door of the inn in this watercolour.

Provenance: Sir Joseph Banks; by descent to Sir William Knatchbull; Christie's, London, 23 May 1876, lot 45; purchased by the Royal Librarian, Richard Holmes, for the Royal Collection (30 gs.)

Literature: Oppé 37; RL 14559

PAUL SANDBY (c.1730-1809)

46 *Windsor Castle from the North,* c.1770

262 x 519 mm.
Pen and black ink and watercolour over pencil. (For original unfaded colour see green edges, formerly hidden by mount or frame, lower left).

Paul Sandby's views of Windsor include a number taken from the River Thames, which separates the towns of Windsor (on the left bank in this watercolour) and Eton (on the right). Windsor Castle, built on raised ground, occupies the main part of this picture. The Round Tower, with its tall flagstaff, is shown before its transformation (and heightening) by Wyatville in the early nineteenth century (cf.No.48). The upper outline of St George's Chapel can just be made out above the two horses on the riverside path. Details such as the cart drawn by three horses in front of the wall vertically below the Round Tower should not be missed.

From their broad proportions, we must assume that both Nos.45 and 46 were made to be framed and displayed on a wall. Carefully protected, with material hanging over the frames, and layers of curtaining screening the harmful rays on sunlight from the windows, No.45 has retained much of its original crispness and delicate colouring. Unfortunately the same has not been the case with No.46, which may be slightly later in date, c.1770.

Provenance: purchased from Lady Ponsonby, November 1955

Literature: RL17807

JAMES DUFFIELD HARDING (1797-1863)

47   *The Palace of Holyroodhouse,* c.1850

265 x 415 mm.
Watercolour and bodycolour
heightened with white over traces of pencil
on buff paper.

The Palace of Holyroodhouse, on the outskirts of Edinburgh is still in use today as the monarch's residence during her visits to Edinburgh, the capital city of Scotland. In Queen Victoria's reign it served as a convenient stopping-off point on the long journey north to Balmoral Castle in Aberdeenshire. The Queen first stayed at Holyroodhouse in 1850. This watercolour gives a good impression of the clutter of miscellaneous buildings facing the imposing entrance front of the Palace. Holyroodhouse owes its origins to the Abbey, founded in 1128, and has acted as a royal residence - first for Scottish monarchs and (from 1603) of the monarchs of Scotland and England - since that time. The Palace buildings are mainly of the sixteenth and seventeenth centuries.

Queen Victoria's Souvenir Albums in which No.47 was formerly mounted, housed watercolours of the journeys made by the Queen and Prince Albert from 1840. They spent most Sunday evenings and two evenings a week, whenever possible, arranging their growing collection of drawings. During the next twenty years nine volumes were filled with over 600 watercolours, including more than 100 views of Scotland. They were bound in dark blue leather, 'with VR and the Crown upon them' (D. Millar, *Queen Victorias's Life in the Scottish Highlands*, London, 1985, p.9).

Provenance: commissioned by Queen Victoria for her Souvenir Albums (vol.V, 1849-52, p.36)

Literature: RL19566

JOSEPH NASH (1809-1878)

48 *Sunday Morning in the Lower Ward, 1846*

330 x 473 mm.
Watercolour and bodycolour heightened with white over traces of pencil. Signed and dated lower right: *Joseph Nash. 1846.*

A (handcoloured) lithograph (by T. McLean) of this view of the Lower Ward, Windsor Castle, looking eastwards towards the Round Tower, was included as Plate I in Nash's *Views of the Interior and Exterior of Windsor Castle*, published in 1848. The plate is entitled: 'Lower Ward, with view of St George's Chapel and Round Tower. Sunday Afternoon' (sic). However the accompanying letterpress confirms that 'It represents the Ward previous to the opening of St George's Chapel for Divine Service on Sunday morning. The attributes of the spot, viz. a troop of choristers, the military on duty, and the public waiting for admission into the Royal Chapel, give animation and brilliancy to the tableau, and enhance its value as a representation of the pleasing scene'.

Wyatville's remodelling of Windsor Castle included the Private and State Apartments, the Round Tower (shown in the centre background with its additional storey), and the Military Knight's Houses (on the right). At his death in 1840 part of the Lower Ward remained 'unimproved', and work was continued on the Salisbury Tower, the Guard Room, etc. by Salvin in the 1860s. The pile of masonry fragments in the foreground provides some indication of work still under way.

To the left a group of choirboys and choristers proceed from the entrance to the Horseshoe Cloister towards the south door of St George's Chapel.

Joseph Nash's publication on Windsor Castle was chiefly concerned with Wyatville's work there. Although it was made with Queen Victoria's express permission and was dedicated to the Queen, most of the watercolours on which the illustrations were based appear to have remained with the artist, rather than being passed to Queen Victoria. This particular watercolour was acquired (with other works of the same series) earlier this century.

Provenance: March 1937 purchased for the Royal Collection

Literature: RL19780

JOSEPH NASH (1809-1878)

49 *Buckingham Palace,* 1846

277 x 402 mm.
Watercolour and bodycolour heightened with white, over traces of pencil.
Signed and dated lower left: *J. Nash. 1846.*

Verso. Slight pencil sketch of the receding left wall of St George's Hall, Windsor Castle.

Following its purchase by George III in 1762, Buckingham House was repeatedly adapted and extended so that by Queen Victoria's reign it could truly be described as a Palace. The structure shown in this watercolour preserves the main block of the original house (behind the central pediment supported by paired columns) as the core of a U-shaped building with two vast flanking wings. However, the Queen's growing family ensured that this solution (devised by Nash for George IV) was soon found to be inadequate, and Edward Blore (who had succeeded Nash as the architect in charge at Buckingham House in 1830) was therefore commissioned to build a new eastern block, as a result of which the former 'cour d'Honneur' became an internal courtyard. The eastern range was added in 1847, the year after the execution of this watercolour.

In the same year, 1847, the 'Marble Arch' to the east of the Palace was dismantled, prior to its reassembly four years later at the north-east corner of Hyde Park (where it still stands). The arch, built to commemorate the British victories on land and sea in the Napoleonic campaign, had only been completed earlier in 1846, following numerous problems that had arisen since the laying of the foundation stone in 1828.

St James's Park provided grazing for cattle and sheep for many centuries. The ducks and swans in the foreground can still be found in profusion on the lake in the Park.

The slight sketch on the *verso* was uncovered during conservation work on the watercolour in 1986. It appears to be related to Nash's watercolour of St George's Hall, Windsor Castle (RL 19790), painted as a record of the banquet in honour of King Louis Philippe's visit to Windsor on 11th October 1844. Two years later the artist evidently decided to use the other side of this otherwise blank sheet of paper.

Provenance: commissioned by Queen Victoria for her Souvenir Albums (vol. III, 1845-46, p. 36)

Literature: RL 19892

WILLIAM SIMPSON (1823-1899)

50 *Balmoral Castle from the North West, 1882*

290 x 443 mm.
Watercolour and bodycolour heightened with white, over traces of pencil.
Inscribed, signed and dated, lower left: *Balmoral. W. Simpson. 1882.*

Balmoral Castle, Aberdeenshire, was first visited by Queen Victoria in September 1848, by which time the lease on the house and estate had been acquired (as Prince Albert's private property). In Autumn 1852 the freehold was purchased, and plans were already under way to demolish the old house and build a new one, nearer the River Dee, to the designs of William Smith. By 1856 the new Castle was complete. Its appearance has not changed substantially in the intervening years, and Simpson's watercolour therefore records both the work of the 1850s and the building of today, which is still much used by the Royal Family.

William Simpson's involvement with the Royal Family dated back to 1855-6, when the Queen allowed his book on the Crimean War *(Illustrations of the War in the East)* to be dedicated to her. He covered the Prince of Wales's tour of India (1875-76) for the *Illustrated London News* and then in 1881 was invited to Balmoral to paint a series of watercolours of the Castle and surrounding area. As the resulting pictures are all dated 1882, Simpson must have completed them some time after the visit (see Millar, *op. cit.* in No. 47, p. 133).

Provenance: commissioned by Queen Victoria

Literature: RL19529

Artists' Biographies

Benozzo Gozzoli
Florence c. 1421 - Pistoia 1497

Benozzo was trained as a painter but in his early years also worked for the sculptor Ghiberti. He is chiefly known as Fra Angelico's principal assistant from 1447 to the latter's death in 1455, working with him in Rome and Orvieto. After his master's death Benozzo resided in Rome, Florence, San Gimignano, and latterly chiefly at Pisa. The majority of his work is in fresco.

School of Andrea Mantegna
? Isola di Carturo 1431-Mantua 1506

A precocious child, Mantegna was adopted by the Paduan painter and antiquary Francesco Squarcione and joined the Paduan guild between 1441 and 1445. In 1453 he married the daughter of the Venetian painter Jacopo Bellini, and was thus brother-in-law to both Gentile and Giovanni Bellini. In 1459/60 Mantegna moved to Mantua where he worked for the remainder of his life, apart from a visit to Rome 1488/90. The work of Florentine artists in Padua during Mantegna's formative years, and the antiquarian interests of his patrons in both Padua and Mantua, combined to produce his distinctive classicizing style. This was soon disseminated through the medium of woodcuts and engravings, including some from Mantegna's own hand.

Pietro Vannucci, called Perugino
Città della Pieve c. 1445 - Fontignano 1523

There is little secure evidence about the artist's training, which may have included instruction from Piero della Francesca.
In 1472 Perugino is listed among the company of St Luke in Florence. It is possible that he was a pupil of Verrocchio (as was Leonardo). Perugino's first important work is in the Sistine Chapel alongside paintings by Filippino and others (1481/82). Thereafter he painted in Florence and in and around Perugia, the town which gave him his name. Raphael appears to have been his pupil. Perugino's work, characterized by decorative and sometimes vapid gestures and expressions, painted with great technical proficiency, was widely popular during his lifetime.

Leonardo da Vinci
Vinci 1452 - Amboise 1519

Leonardo matriculated as a painter in Florence in 1472, following a period of training in the studio of the sculptor-painter Andrea del Verrocchio in whose house he was still living in 1476. In c.1482 he transferred to the Sforza court in Milan, where he worked as architect, engineer, court painter and sculptor (Sforza monuments, *Last Supper*, etc.).
In 1500 Leonardo returned to Florence (via Venice), where he was chiefly resident until 1506. Thereafter he returned to Milan (until 1513), before moving to Rome (1513-16) and finally France where he lived (and died) at the Chateau of Cloux near Amboise. Very few works of painting, sculpture and architecture by Leonardo have survived. In consequence his drawings, of which 600 are in the Royal Collection, are particularly important. They reveal the extraordinary breadth of his interests and his constantly probing mind, which led to much artistic experimentation. Recognised as a genius in his own lifetime, Leonardo's work had an immediate impact on the development of later Renaissance art, both north and south of the Alps.

ARTISTS' BIOGRAPHIES

FILIPPINO LIPPI
? Prato 1457/8 - Florence 1504

The illegitimate son of the painter Fra Filippo Lippi (c.1406-69), a monk in holy orders at the Carmine, Florence. Following a childhood spent in Prato, Filippino was with his father in Spoleto in 1467 and after his father's death entered the Florentine workshop of Fra Filippo's pupils, Sandro Botticelli. In 1484 Filippino was commissioned to complete Masaccio's fresco cycle in the Brancacci chapel of the Carmine, revealing the strong influence of his father's later mystical works, and the linear style of Botticelli. He worked in Rome from 1488, executing a number of important fresco cycles and altarpieces, and developing a more substantial figurative style.

MICHELANGELO BUONARROTI, called MICHELANGELO
Caprese 1475 - Rome 1564

Michelangelo was born near Arezzo and trained in the Florentine studio of the painter Ghirlandaio. For most of his life he was active as painter, sculptor and architect, chiefly in Florence and Rome. His early study of the newly-formed collections of classical antiquities, and of the works of earlier artists such as Giotto and Masaccio, led to the development of Michelangelo's monumental figure style. His frescoes in the Sistine Chapel (1508-12, and 1536-41) were revolutionary in scale and in the articulation of the picture space. Michelangelo's figures have a new tension and vigour, in painting and sculpture alike. In the field of architecture, in which he was chiefly active in his later years, his work was likewise based on classical forms, and was influential both in his own lifetime and for succeeding centuries.

RAFFAELLO SANTI, called RAPHAEL
Urbino 1483 - Rome 1520

Raphael's first artistic instruction was provided by his father, Giovanni Santi, a painter in Urbino. By 1500 he was already producing highly competent works, reflecting the influence of central Italian artists such as Signorelli, Pintoricchio, and particularly Perugino, whose pupil he may have been. In Florence (for much of the period 1504-08) he encountered the art of Leonardo and Michelangelo, before moving to Rome c.1508/9. In his work in fresco in the Vatican *Stanze* he evolved a new narrative style, the influence of which can be felt to our own time. Raphael also painted a number of highly influential small-scale works, both religious and secular. He was active as an architect and archaeologist in Rome. In his later works he was helped by his assistants and pupils, who completed several projects after his early death in 1520.

SEBASTIANO DEL PIOMBO
?Venice c.1485 - Rome 1547

Sebastiano received his first artistic instruction in his native Venice from the aged Giovanni Bellini and then from Giorgione, on whom Sebastiano's early style was dependent. But his residence in Rome from 1511 led to a gradual change in style. Michelangelo supplied him with designs to assist him with a number of compositions. During the decade following Raphael's death (1520) Sebastiano was considered the leading painter in Rome. After his appointment to the lucrative office of 'Piombo' (Keeper of the Papal Seal) in 1531 he painted very little. The sixteenth-century artistic biographer Vasari considered that Sebastiano's greatest works were portraits.

ARTISTS' BIOGRAPHIES

Francesco de'Rossi, called Salviati — Florence 1510 - Rome 1563

Trained in Florence by Andrea del Sarto, by 1531 he was working in Rome under the patronage of Cardinal Giovanni Salviati, from whom he took his name. He was active chiefly in Florence and Rome, visiting Venice 1539-40 and Fontainebleau 1554-55. Salviati worked in a variety of different artistic media, but is chiefly known as the painter of large-scale fresco cycles, packed with historical detail, arranged with typically Mannerist complexity and artificiality and depending on the works of both Raphael and Michelangelo.

Lelio Orsi — Novellara c.1511 - Novellara 1587

The career and œuvre of this artist, whose name was mentioned by neither Vasari nor Baldinucci, are still only scantily documented. Orsi's gravestone at Novellara (inscribed by his son) records him as great in architecture, greater in painting, and greatest of all in draughtsmanship. He was active as a painter at Reggio nell'Emilia in 1536 and 1544, in Venice in 1553, and by December 1554 in Rome. From 1545 to 1552, and after 1559, he was apparently continuously resident in Novellara. A single signed and dated drawing has been used to built up a body of paintings and drawings attributed to this mysterious artist.

Albrecht Dürer — Nuremberg 1471 - Nuremberg 1528

Dürer (who had a precocious talent) trained initially under his father as a goldsmith, but was apprenticed to the Nuremberg painter Michael Wohlgemut in 1486. Throughout his life he travelled extensively. His visits to Italy (particularly Venice) in 1494/5 and 1505/7 were vital to his artistic progress, bringing him into direct contact with the latest developments in Italian Renaissance art. The wide dissemination of Dürer's engravings and woodcuts was crucial in spreading the influence of Italian art throughout Northern Europe. The majority of Dürer's work is both signed and dated, from his first drawn self-portrait of 1484. His development can be traced in various media, and through both religious and secular works.

Hans Holbein the Younger — Augsburg 1497/8 - London 1543

The younger son of an artist of the same name, who provided his first training. Before finally settling in Basel in 1519 Holbein's travels may have taken him to Italy. He was in France in 1524, and in 1526 was reported to be embarking for England in search of work, owing to the current religious troubles in Basel. Apart from a return visit to Basel 1528-32, the remainder of Holbein's life was spent in England. He first arrived there owing to the links between scholars in England and those on the continent (particularly Erasmus) for whom Holbein had worked in Basel. Holbein introduced the art of the Renaissance to England, chiefly through his portraits and decorative works. There was little demand for the religious paintings on which his reputation had first been established.

Augustin Hirschvogel — Nuremberg 1503 - Vienna 1553

The son of a leading stained-glass painter, working in the new decorative style and using the vocabulary introduced by Dürer, Augustin Hirschvogel spent his first thirty years in his native Nuremberg. He was trained by his father, and himself became a talented stained-glass painter and draughtsman. Hirschvogel is best known for his etchings, which were almost all the product of his last decade, spent in Vienna.

ARTISTS' BIOGRAPHIES

LUDOVICO CARRACCI
Bologna 1555 - Bologna 1619

Ludovico was the teacher and cousin of Agostino and Annibale Carracci, with whom he established the Carracci Academy in Bologna 1585/6, at which most of the major Bolognese artists of the next generation were trained (eg. Domenichino, Reni and Guercino). During his maturity (and particularly after the departure of Annibale for Rome in 1595, and the death of Agostino in 1602) Ludovico was based chiefly in Bologna but also worked in Rome and Piacenza. His art therefore remained largely dependent on the examples of Correggio and Tintoretto, rather than following the innovative route pioneered by his cousins.

ANNIBALE CARRACCI
Bologna 1560 - Roma 1609

Annibale was the youngest and most talented of the Carracci, brother of Agostino and cousin of Ludovico, who taught him. Following a visit to Parma c.1585, and contact with major works by Correggio, his early Mannerist style evolved and became more naturalistic. Shortly thereafter he visited Venice, and came into contact with the art of Titian and Veronese. The fame of the Carracci frescoes in the Palazzi Fava and Magnani, Bologna, was doubtless responsible for Annibale's invitation to Rome in 1595 to decorate the Palazzo Farnese. The ceiling of the Gallery there (c.1597-1603/4) is a crucial monument in the development of the Baroque style, clearly demonstrating a three-fold debt to classical antiquity, to Raphael and to Michelangelo. Annibale's oeuvre also includes a number of independent paintings, with sacred and profane subject matter, in which landscape sometimes occupies an important position. During his last four years spent in Rome, Annibale was beset by illness.

GUIDO RENI
Bologna 1575 - Bologna 1642

After an initial apprenticeship with the Flemish painter Denys Calvaert, Reni joined the Carracci Academy 1594/5 and painted his first public work *(Coronation of the Virgin)*. In around 1602 he moved to Rome, but returned on numerous occasions to his native Bologna, and settled there permanently in 1614. Reni painted numerous frescoes and altar-pieces in both cities, with an elegant flowing line and often incorporating a highly charged religious feeling. Like the Carracci, Reni had an active workshop and numerous pupils.

GIOVANNI FRANCESCO BARBIERI, called GUERCINO
Cento 1591-Bologna 1666

The main formative influence for Guercino's style was Ludovico Carracci, whose Academy he attended in nearby Bologna. After early visits to Venice (1618) and Ferrara (1619 and 1620), Guercino was invited to Rome by Pope Gregory XV (1621). With its dramatic dynamism and unified picture space his fresco of *Aurora* (1621-3) for the Casino Ludovisi marks the beginnings of the High Baroque. Following the Pope's death in 1623 Guercino returned to Cento and established a studio there. In the early 1640s, after Reni's death, he transferred to Bologna where he soon became the leading painter. 'Guercino' (meaning squint) was originally Barbieri's nickname. His prodigious output of drawings, mainly in pen and wash, were extremely popular with British collectors.

ARTISTS' BIOGRAPHIES

CARLO MARATTA
Camerano 1625 – Rome 1713

Born near Ancona (on the Adriatic coastline), Maratta was sent to Rome at the age of 11 to develop his artistic talent. He entered the studio of Andrea Sacchi and befriended the theorist Pietro Bellori, their combined enthusiasm being for the more classical styles of Raphael and Annibale Carracci rather than the charged emotion of the High Baroque style personified by Bernini. Following Sacchi's death (1661) Maratta gradually rose to become the leading painter in Rome, acting as head of the Academy of St Luke from 1664, producing altarpieces and decorative schemes for all the major churches and numerous portraits. In addition he worked on several sculptural projects.

GIOVANNI BENEDETTO CASTIGLIONE
Genoa c.1610 – Mantua 1663/5

Castiglione's early training with two local Genoese artists was supplemented by a period in Van Dyck's Genoese studio (1621-7). In the 1630s he moved to Rome (and briefly to Naples), where he was influenced both by the antiquarian activities of the artists working for Cassiano dal Pozzo, and by the early Roman work of Poussin. Thereafter he returned to Genoa (1640-7), Rome (1647-51) and then Mantua, Venice and Genoa again. His many-faceted style includes echoes of the work of Rembrandt, Rubens, Bassano and Poussin. But in both subject-matter and technique Castiglione was a highly original artist. His 'oil drawings' and monotypes are alone in their time.

NICOLAS POUSSIN
Les Andelys 1594 – Rome 1665

Poussin received his first training in Normandy, before moving to Paris in 1612. His earliest known works are the drawings illustrating Ovid's *Metamorphoses* (c.1623), which were commissioned by the Italian poet G. B. Marino. In 1624 Poussin travelled to Rome (via Venice) and apart from a visit to Paris 1640-42 he was resident in Rome for the rest of his life. Poussin's style was formed on the basis of the combined influences of the Antique, Raphael, Titian, and contemporary Bolognese painters. From the 1640s the subject matter of his work was almost exclusively pious and stoical. Poussin's art was profoundly intellectual, and was based on his interest in artistic theory, philosophy, ancient history and religion. He was a personal friend of his fellow-countryman Claude Lorrain, but although their artistic paths crossed on various occasions, they developed in very different directions.

CLAUDE GELLEE, LE LORRAIN
Chamagne (Vosges) 1600 – Rome 1682

Claude travelled to Italy as a boy and received his first artistic training from the landscape painter Agostino Tassi, but he was also influenced by Northern masters such as Elsheimer and the Brills. By 1627, after travels through Italy and France, Claude had settled in Rome where he remained for the rest of his life, working both for Italian and for French visitors. His *Liber Veritatis* (London, British Museum) provides 195 drawn records of his paintings from the 1630s onwards, testifying to his popularity and professionalism. His pictures are mainly landscapes, views of rivers, coastal scenes or harbours suffused with the light of the rising or setting sun.

ARTISTS' BIOGRAPHIES

ANTONIO CANALE, called CANALETTO
Venice 1697 - Venice 1768

Initially Canaletto appears to have followed the career of his father, as a theatrical designer. He may have visited Rome c.1719. Canaletto's independent works date from the early 1720s and he soon established a reputation for the production of bright and brilliant topographical views of his native Venice. The main influence on his art was Luca Carlevaris, whose paintings (and particularly etchings) first popularised Venetian views. By 1730 he was being patronized by Joseph Smith (British Consul from 1744), and his ties with British collectors were of great importance. He visited England 1746-50 and in the early 1750s, mainly because the regular flow of Grand Tourists to Venice had been interrupted by war.

GIOVANNI BATTISTA PIAZZETTA
Venice 1683 - Venice 1754

The son of a Venetian sculptor and wood carver, Piazzetta's main artistic training took place in Bologna, under G. M. Crespi. There he acquired his fine sense of chiaroscuro, and studied drawing in the tradition of the Carracci Academy. By 1711 Piazzetta had returned to Venice, where he remained for the rest of his life. He produced paintings (on canvas, never murals) for a number of churches, and also portraits and book illustrations. In 1750 he was elected Director of the Venetian Academy.

PAUL SANDBY
Nottingham c.1730 - London 1809

The younger brother of the draughtsman and architect Thomas Sandby, with whom he travelled from their native Nottingham to London c.1742. Paul's early training was as a military draughtsman and cartographer in the Drawing Office of the Tower. He was sent to Scotland to work as a draughtsman on the Highland Survey (1746-51) and then joined his brother at Windsor, the subject of many of his finest watercolours and prints. He was a founder member of the Royal Academy and exhibited oils and bodycolours there throughout his life. But his chief importance lies in his role as teacher both at the Royal Military Academy, Woolwich (1768-96), and in private lessons to numerous pupils who included influential amateurs such as Lord Harcourt and Sir Watkin Williams Wynn. His travels through Wales with the latter, resulting in series of aquatint views, were also important for the development of landscape painting.

JAMES DUFFIELD HARDING
Deptford 1797 - Barnes, Surrey 1863

The son of John Harding, engraver and drawing master, who had been taught by Paul Sandby. Following tuition from his father and from Samuel Prout, J. D. Harding was first apprenticed to the engraver Charles Pye. After a year he left Pye to concentrate on watercolour painting. He exhibited in a number of different contexts, including the Royal Academy (from 1811), and the Old Watercolour Society. Harding's oeuvre consists chiefly of landscapes and topography in watercolours, but he also worked in oils and as an engraver and topographer. He visited Italy on several occasions from 1824, travelled to the Rhine in 1834 and 1837, to Normandy in 1842, and to Gibraltar. He was active as a teacher throughout his life, and numbered John Ruskin among his pupils. Ruskin considered Harding 'unquestionably the greatest master of foliage in Europe'.

ARTISTS' BIOGRAPHIES

Joseph Nash
Great Marlow 1809 - London 1878

The son of a clergyman (who kept a school at Croydon) and pupil of the architectural draughtsman A.C. Pugin, with whom he travelled to France in the late 1820s. His work consists chiefly of picturesque architectural subjects, illustrations and genre scenes, and romantically peopled domestic interiors. There are few works after 1854, when Nash suffered an attack of 'brain fever'. He is best-known as a lithographer, both of his own compositions and views (eg. *Architecture of the Middle Ages, Mansions of England, Scotland Delineated, Windsor Castle*, and the *Great Exhibition*), and of those of others (eg. Wilkie).

William Simpson
Glasgow 1823 - London 1899

Simpson's early training was as an architect-engineer, then as a lithographer, in Scotland. From 1851 to 1866 he worked for the London printing firm, Day & Son, and later for the *Illustrated London News*. He was sent to the Baltic and then the Crimea to record naval and military events, and was thus one of the first war artists. Later assignments took him to Circassia, India, Tibet, Russia, Jerusalem, Abyssinia, China, Japan, America, Asia Minor and Afghanistan. His work from these travels was chiefly intended for reproduction in black and white, but he was also a fine watercolourist, and occasionally painted in oils.

Index of Artists

41–3	CANALETTO (Antonio Canale)	33	MARATTA, Carlo
29	CARRACCI, Annibale	15, 16	MICHELANGELO (Michelangelo Buonarroti)
28	CARRACCI, Ludovico	48, 49	NASH, Joseph
34	CASTIGLIONE, Giovanni Benedetto	21	ORSI, Lelio
22, 23	DÜRER, Albrecht	3	PERUGINO (Pietro Vannucci)
1	GOZZOLI, Benozzo (attributed to)	44	PIAZZETTA, Giovanni Battista
31, 32	GUERCINO (Giovanni Barbieri)	35–7	POUSSIN, Nicolas
47	HARDING, James Duffield	17, 18	RAPHAEL (Raffaello Santi)
27	HIRSCHVOGEL, Augustin	30	RENI, Guido
24–6	HOLBEIN, Hans the Younger	20	SALVIATI (Francesco de' Rossi)
4–13	LEONARDO da Vinci	45, 46	SANDBY, Paul
14	LIPPI, Filippino	19	SEBASTIANO del Piombo
38–40	LORRAIN, Claude Gellée, Le	50	SIMPSON, William
2	MANTEGNA, Andrea (School of)